We Are USCO

Sounds good, doesn't it? Kind of friendly. Very patriotic. Lean. Maybe even a little bit mean. We should know. USCO is us. And we've decided to let you in on just what we are. The "U" is for United. The "S" stands for States—all 50 of them, plus a few new ones you don't know about yet. Best of all, "CO" is for Company, as in money. Our name may be new, but everyone has met us. We're what used to be known as the Government of the United States of America.

USCO does much more, though, than give free dairy products to everyone. We're the people who service you. Twenty-four hours a day. Every night as you roll happily over at the end of yet another full day's servicing, we're still hard at work. Scouring the planet for today's necessities and tomorrow's treats. Why do we do it? Because we're sweet on you, America. You are our *main squeeze*.

We wish we could keep things as simple as just saying "We love you." But it's a complicated world out there. USCO is not alone. An extremely unpleasant bunch of pcoplc wants to take away all the nice things we've given you. The bully's name is MOSCO. But don't let this get you down— we also have some friends. These friends, although we regret to say some don't know what friends are for, are called THEMCO. MOSCO wants to take THEMCO away from USCO. They don't stand a chance.

USCO has something that nobody else can get. He's a nice old gent we gave a helping hand to a few years back. Today he's the most popular guy on the planet. His name is Ronald Reagan. Sure, he's a little bit slow on the uptake (the poor old geezer actually thinks he's the president of the company!). But he's pulled off a couple of good ones recently. And we know he's going to take just dandy care of you, at least for as long as he can stay awake.
So without further ado:
Heeeeeeeeeeeeere's
Ronnie!

The Reagan Report

By USCO Parody, Inc.
A Dolphin Book
Doubleday & Company, Inc.
Garden City, New York
1984

Library of Congress Cataloging in Publication Data
Main entry under title:
The Reagan Report

  1. United States—Politics and government—
Anecdotes, facetiae, satire, etc. 2. Corporation
reports—Anecdotes, facetiae, satire, etc. I. Cohn,
Peter, II. Kaestle, David. III. Title: The Reagan
Report   PN6231.P6U82 1984   818′.5407
84-4100   ISBN 0-385-19516-8

Letter From the President

My fellow Americans, it's been a great four years. Americans are walking taller and talking louder all over the world. Sometimes I can hear them myself. All over this nation, people who have something nice to say are saying it—and they're saying it in American, thank you very much. And people who don't have any-

Mr. & Mrs. Pete Jennings, Waco, Texas

A nice man who really loves America

like that, it just seems to me that no one is going to stop this country from happening.

When I look back over what we've accomplished in the past four years, I get so excited I don't have any trouble paying attention. I'm pretty darn popular these days! Our White House staff has been receiving letters, postcards, and hundreds of other kinds of writing, too, all running two-to-one in favor of what we claim to be doing. That's called "patriotism."

The American people are tired of walking across the street every time they see their President headed their way. Well, I've tried to do something about that. I want to be remembered as the first President who didn't just bore people with a lot of "political" talk. I mean, who wants to listen to someone talk, talk, talk about treaties with Germany and so on? Let the intellectuals get it from the newspaper, if they're so interested! What I've given people is that enjoyment, that ability, where the American people can stand right there in the middle of the road and wave proudly whenever the Presidential motorcade drives through. And yes, sometimes I'll wave back. What I'm talking about is not ignoring people I don't even know, because that's what a President sometimes has to do.

Not only am I better off, but a broad range of Americans are better off too. Of course, it hasn't been done without some sacrifices and some corner cutting. You know, when I first got here, there was a man in the White House whose whole job was just saying "Good morning, Mr. President" whenever I walked by! Or "Good night," if it was in the night. Well, frankly, that's just a waste of your tax dollars. So now I have him tell me the sports news, too.

And I'm sure there are a couple of naysayers out there claiming that just because I'm President I don't have to do without once in a while. But let me tell you: One of Nancy and I's favorite things when we lived in California

thing nice to say—well, they're not saying anything at all, which is their right. But there's more to it than that.

Why, just the other day I got this note from Sally Wirth, a second grader in Mrs. Betty Willits's second-grade class. I'd like to share it with you, because I think this little girl really knows what she's talking about. She wrote: "I hope when you have the Easter egg hunt on the White House lawn next year, there aren't any terrorists peeking through the fence with bombs shaped like Easter eggs. I don't want you to get mixed up and put a bomb in your basket by mistake." Well, Sally, whoever you are, I want to thank you. Because when second graders really care about their President

Everybody wants to show the flag! Mable Fitho, Chicago

was water-skiing. Well, if you look around Washington, maybe *you'll* see a lot of places to water-ski. All I can say is, it looks more like pavement to me. If you want to try it, go ahead! Just don't tell me I don't know how to make sacrifices for my country.

Oh, I know we have a long way to go. But Americans have never been one to shrink from having a go at having to go along with ...well, let me put it this way: I recently heard about a woman in Pittsburgh who went into a supermarket to buy an apple. Well, she bought the apple—and the grocer gave her back fourteen cents in change. And that, for your information, is a true story.

A list of our accomplishments could go on for longer than a person could concentrate without a nap. But it all comes down to one thing. Money. You can't spell "America" without all the letters in "money." Well, actually, you can. But you wouldn't want to. And neither would I.

That's why, sometime last year, we went to all the trouble of incorporating the U.S. Government in the state of Delaware. We're USCO now. And that's why we've published this annual report.

Now I firmly believe that Government shouldn't try to act like a publisher. Because then you'd have publishers trying to act like Government to get even, and you'd have a situation where the Abner Doubleday Company would do what we're doing, and spend $1.4

Today's young people are wonderful —Tommy LaPorte, Brooklyn. N.Y.

trillion to develop an edible helicopter. And Harcourt Brace Jehosaphat would have to start its own summer camp for death squads. And that's just plain inefficient.

Not only that, once Government starts publishing things, the next thing you know you've got mandatory airbags and mandatory strangers having to kiss everyone they pass, and jails for horses and...I don't think I have to say this...Communist tyranny. As Karl Marx himself wrote, if I can remember it without my glasses, "Communism is bad for business, because we're atheists, and we hate everything."

We made for you a symbol of dignity and courage.
The Roselli Family, Ardmore, Pa.

Well, that may go over big in Moscow, but it won't play in Peoria. Now it just so happens that I did play in Peoria once. I played baseball. And I don't mind telling you something else: When I looked around that playing field, I don't remember seeing Karl Marx. Anywhere. And you surely don't need to put on your glasses when you're remembering something.

I know you'll all back me up on this, because some time ago, you may remember, I went before the American people to explain about the "window of vulnerability" that existed between us and the Soviets. Well, the American people responded. They said one thing to the enemies of freedom, and they said it loud and clear: The United States doesn't "do" windows.

I mean, unless you break them with a good old American curve ball. Of course, many of us believe that baseball is just business played outdoors. Because you've got a leather mitt, and that's like your briefcase. You've got a bat, and that corresponds analogously to your fountain pen. And so on. Now, no one can accuse this Administration of playing hardball with business! But even in Delaware, where Government and business are the same thing, there are rules about corporations, and publishing little books. And we want to give every appearance of abiding by those rules.

That's why we've put together this report about USCO. Oh, I know a lot of you will think "Why doesn't he just give us nerve gas? I can't read this. I can't read anything." Believe me, I'm the same way. But it just so happens that we have in this nation a group of people who you pay to read things for you. These people are called lawyers—they "law" for "yer." I suggest you hire yourself one to read this book to you. And if you can't... well, maybe that'll give you some idea of what it's like to live behind an iron curtain.

In these pages you'll find that Americans

Oct 27, 1983

Dear Ron;
What a noisy damn place this is — if I was woken up once last night by gunfire I was awoken a dozen times. Saw the blown up Marine h.q. this morning. Quel mess! Except for the stretchers, it looked like a big trash dump. But the commander says he's very sorry about the bomb thing — and I believe he sincerely is. Over a bottle of J. Walker last eve he and I decided these guys must be pulled out. Next February, say, the Marines go offshore — call it a "redeployment" or somesuch. Then a month later you just ship them the hell out. (Gemayel seemed a little peed when I ran this by him today. But

The President
White House
Washington, D.C.

N.B.D, I don't think.)
Be back Mon. Cheers
George B.

are busy working again, because we know that as long as USCO stays in business, at least somebody, somewhere, will have a job. In fact, that happens to be the role of the President. Apart from all his other duties… diplomatic goings-on and signing checks and balances for paying bills the Congress sends over…the President, I suppose in a symbolic function, who serves, I mean, his job, his role —the President has a job. He is the President. And that stands as a symbol, to all Americans, of what is possible. Because I assure you: It is possible to have a job.

Now, I'm not saying that every man can be President. No, I'm referring to the symbolic function of the President, as being the Chief Employee of the United States. He's a success story, just as a tall, strong money tree is to that little new-minted penny. An example of what it's like to be employed.

This, as far as I can tell, is what USCO is all about. Of course, there are those who claim that only the rich have benefited from USCO and its policies and programs. Well, that simply isn't so. Their tailors have benefited. Their drivers have benefited. Their "help" have benefited. And maybe that's a lesson we can all learn from the wealthy: They're people who are not too proud to ask for help. And they're not too poor to hire it.

I'd like to close with one little story I heard

the other day that I felt should be shared. Recently I heard of a woman in a small town in Ohio. It seems her husband had been out of work for almost eighteen months. He took his hunting rifle down off its rack, and, well, he went out in the backyard and blew his, well, brains out. But the story doesn't end there. Because that woman went into the backyard, stood over her husband's remains and recited the Pledge of Allegiance. And he came back to life. His head was good as new, and he got a job the next day. This is a true story. And they gave him a new car, too.

Now, you're welcome to help yourself to the jar, but leave the orange ones for me. They're cantaloupe. And they're my favorite. Nancy likes the pink ones.

My fellow Presidents, God bless you and, well, God *bless* you.

Ronald Reagan

Ronald Wilson Reagan

Chief Executive Officer

Highlights

Ronald Reagan's first term: A never-ending succession of Presidential triumphs!

Just after being sworn in, Ronald Reagan sings his Inaugural Song: "Yo! Ho! I'm the President now....When folks look at me, they'll say Wow!"

A Federal Cheese Warden prepares portions of still-warm cottage cheese for senior citizens in Corpus Christi, Texas.

"Do you really believe that angels are watching us all the time, even when we're getting dressed?" President Reagan asks the Pontiff.

Ferdinand Marcos adopts the Reagan coif. The President is moved by this homage.

The President subs as an air traffic controller. "This is easy," he says as he "brings down" a 747.

Above: In his first official act, the President frees the 52 Americans being held hostage in Teheran. The night of their return, they are greeted by the Reagans at a celebratory gala. "The experience has changed us forever," say the hostages.

Right: "Darn tootin' fleas. I wouldn't sit on this thing with three saddles."

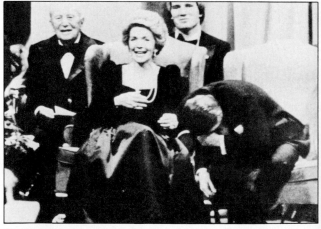

At the first John Hinckley Commemorative Pageant, the President and First Lady perform an amusing dramatization of the failed assassination attempt.

There were moments of solemn dignity, and others of lighthearted whimsy.

"Mommy, I love you, and I love your wooden arm," coos the President.

The President suggests to Queen Elizabeth II that she solve the Northern Ireland situation.

A Nuclear Slaughtering Module quickly converts a cow (*above*) into tasty ground beef (*right*).

The First Lady makes headlines in an appearance on *Good Morning America* that marked the first time an American was crowned on network television.

The best defense *is* the Department of Defense. No Libyan hit squad could blast through this baby!

Future MD Ernie Kopple—prior to his rescue by the U.S. Army—conducts an experiment at St. George's Medical College in Grenada.

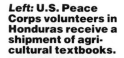

Left: U.S. Peace Corps volunteers in Honduras receive a shipment of agricultural textbooks.

Charles Z. Wick welcomes guests to his Georgetown home.

Left: Cool and calm George Shultz gets a Pentagon briefing on covert activities, NATO readiness and which iron to use on the 12th hole.

Below: At a Harvard symposium, Abraham Lincoln praises President Reagan for aggressively enforcing anti-slavery laws.

A festive nuclear explosion over Switzerland's breathtaking Alp Mountains highlights the 1982 Presidential visit to Europe.

Domestic Affairs
America's Grab-Bag

Most Americans would probably agree that they don't think much about domestic affairs. They probably don't realize that every time someone goes hungry, *that's* a domestic affair. Whenever someone goes homeless, that's another. Women are an entire domestic affair in themselves—and so are farmers. Even trees, birds and Indians somehow fit into the domestic picture.

In fact, almost every American has something to do with domestic affairs. Now that we're in the Government business, we're required to say that it's our job to take care of all of you. It's what they call public relations —just a cost of doing business. We're not saying that makes any sense, but it's one of the reasons we're always so busy. We don't even have the time to stop and wonder... who's taking care of us?

Home ownership has always been the American Dream, and urban denizens everywhere have earned a new sense of self-esteem as a result of our Homeless Improvement Program. More than 20,000 surplus homes have been distributed.

Hunger Programs—Just in Case

It's no accident that the words "welfare" and "warfare" share so many letters. Both can destroy civilization in a matter of minutes, both place tremendous burdens on society, both demand undue amounts of attention from leaders who are already much too pressed for time. In short, neither one of them is "fair."

Yet at least warfare has the advantage of keeping poor people off the streets. Welfare, on the other hand, forces them there—and keeps them so relaxed and well fed that few would survive the first 10 minutes of boot camp.

Clearly America's gone very wrong somewhere. But we're working to make sure the mistakes of previous administrations won't be repeated. We won't rest until the word "welfare" grates as harshly on the American ear as the word "poop."

But getting rid of welfare doesn't mean getting rid of helping people. Although we believe, for example, that there's no such thing as a free school lunch, food is a top priority. Of course Americans are never hungry, but there may be certain lower-income citizens who feel like a snack occasionally— a bit of ketchup soup, perhaps. We've introduced a number of innovative programs to help these people—always bearing in mind that real Americans neither *need* help nor want handouts.

One program is a new national food lottery: Notalotta. To play Notalotta, "poor people" contribute one dollar per family. The winning family is awarded all the food the total will buy. "In this way," says Michael Romney, Notalotta Director, "we can be sure that one family's getting to eat well, at least."

Early efforts to establish Notalotta proved partially unsuccessful. Officials in South Carolina, for example, thinking that the prize was "all the *flour* the total will buy," awarded one family 360 tons of Swansdown,

Say "cheese, cheese, cheese, cheese, cheese!" Shelley Sherman, 11, seems to smile as she gets ready for a surplus cheese lunch at the Whiteworth Middle School in Dayton, Ohio. The cheese costs the taxpayer next to nothing while providing hungry kids with the yellowest food anyone could want.

Thanks to President Reagan's tax cuts, all Americans found a little extra spending money in their pockets. Some displayed laudable public spirit by using part of the windfall to turn their lawns into beautiful, sweeping showcases. Others, unfortunately, were more self-indulgent, squandering their funds on quickly consumed luxury items.

and on another occasion the same officials mistakenly assumed that they themselves were the intended beneficiaries of the food. But once Notalotta survived these minor setbacks, the lottery flourished. Today, "a lotta" people participate in Notalotta.

Food means less to those of the needy who spend most of their time drinking (which is to say, the majority of those who call themselves needy). Yet we could not bring ourselves to turn our backs on these pitiful miscreants. Thanks to a bill passed last year in the Senate, wines such as Thunderbird and Night Train are now fortified with 12 vitamins and iron; three swigs offer the equivalent of a pound of Wonder Bread.

For those who are still unable to fend for themselves, though, there are more than enough soup kitchens at charitable organizations all over the country. Staffed entirely by volunteers, these kitchens offer lazy freeloaders a chance to get full for nothing. It's a laudable effort, and we're doing our best to promote it by helping these volunteer staffs become more selective about whom they serve. Among other things, we've compiled a list of the nation's 10 *truly* needy people:

George Abbot	Tucky Ferguson
Sally Anderson	Lawrence Hamilton
Lucy Chesterfield	Marion Mitchell
Michael Crawford	Douglas Stern
Elaine Delacorte	Julia Whitmore

These 10 people actually need your help. The rest are only looking for handouts.

Voluntarism—The Vestigial Art

Voluntarism used to be thought of as woman's work: rich dowagers teaching slum children how to weave baskets. As one previous President put it, "Volunteer work? That's work done *by* losers *for* losers. Let's raise taxes twenty percent instead."

Today such deplorable attitudes are completely out of date. We now know that volunteer work is a woman's highest calling, and we're doing everything we can to make sure it stays that way.

A two-step program is planned to help encourage American voluntarism. As of January 1985, we will begin providing government incentives to entice more people into doing volunteer work. Active members of the Junior League will receive gold-filled charms suitable for wearing as a pendant or attaching to a bracelet. Hospital volunteers will be awarded diplomas at special ceremonies; even women who work in hospital gift shops will become certified DVMs (Doctors of Volunteer Medicine). Fund-raising volunteers will be "paid" as much Monopoly money as they raise. And women who work in drug-abuse programs will be sent an autographed copy of the First Lady's exercise routine.

Once the incentive program is under way, we will begin implementing its second phase, in which working women—who do not always find time to volunteer—will be required to devote one working day per week to volunteering. "Maybe a couple of women will get fired," says Ray Purdy, chairman of

Margaret Heckler: What could be better than a member of the "fairer sex" in our "fairest" cabinet post, Health and Human Services.

Don't get me wrong. I'm not saying that the poor don't have a hard time. But I think we could all get something out of the story about little Dorothy.

You remember when Dorothy's mean old Auntie Em made her whitewash the back fence. Well, Dorothy didn't feel much like doing it, but she went out there and just pretended whitewashing was the greatest thing that ever happened to her. And by golly if the Scarecrow and the Tin Man didn't think it looked like so much fun that they asked for a turn—and before you know it, the whole fence was done.

That's what I mean when I ask us all to tighten our belts a little. (Not that I really have to—ever since that guy Jody Foster tried to assassinate me, I've been doing exercises to get back in shape. I won't ask you to look at my stomach muscles, but believe me, they're pretty impressive!) No one wants to do it—but maybe if we'd all put a little smile on our face, it would be a little easier. Then, before you know it, the Russians will be so jealous of us they'll pop!

the new program. "But they'll discover the joys of volunteering in the process. And that's something no job could ever replace."

Safety Second

There's really something a little repellent in all the clamor about protecting the public from this and that. Safe cars...safe homes...safe drugs...where does it end? Isn't it a little conceited of everyone to assume that they're all *worth* saving? And even if they are, why are they looking to *us* to save them? True salvation certainly doesn't reside on earth. We can't help but suspect that some people are going to be pretty embarrassed on Judgment Day when they realize what a fuss they were making about *earthly* safety.

Well, the joke will be on them. Still, none of us wants to find a chopped-off finger in

his Big Mac, and it's true that employers shouldn't have to work in a place that's liable to burst into flames at any second. *Some* aspects of temporal safety are worth paying attention to!

Food is one of these. Everyone's heard horror stories about people who fell into the donut machine and were served at a country club banquet the next day. Happily, such tales are now a thing of the past. Every day the Food and Drug Administration works harder to protect you from the food you eat.

Our researchers have discovered, for example, that bone bits, hair fragments and other nonfood by-products are in fact inexpensive and delicious sources of complete protein. "An all-beef hotdog is pretty much what it sounds like," notes the president of Consumer Affairs at the FDA. "But you add some chicken beaks and snouts and stuff in there, and you'll get more protein as well as more fiber."

And so the FDA has become even more demanding in its food standards, revising its requirements to fit the new nutritional knowledge. Beef products are now required by law to contain *at least* 10 percent nonfood "extras." Peanut butter must offer 300 rat hairs per jar unless it is "chunky" style, in which case it must contain more, and regular butter, which is low in protein, must now be supplemented with lard.

We're working to make American cars safer, too. Our newest innovation: voluntary airbags, which will appear in all American cars after January 1, 1986. These sturdy plastic bags may be carried on the lap or stored in the back seat. All the driver needs to do is blow them up and hold them in front of him when he realizes that he is about to have an accident.

New cars will also be provided with small megaphones to enable drivers to warn others. These will be helpful in what used to be considered difficult situations: A polite "I'd rather you didn't tailgate me, please" will go a long way toward preventing an accident.

As for children's car seats, we'd like to

see them abolished before the end of the decade. The safest place for a child is on its parent's lap.

For Weaklings Only

We are committed to eradicating the causes of death everywhere, and we project a death-free United States by the year 2000.

But it is our aim that Americans be, in the words of Benjamin Franklin, "healthy, wealthy, and not a burden to society." Ordinary people should not be obligated to take financial responsibility for those who lack the foresight to stay well.

Among some of our cost-saving health measures, we've introduced a bill in Congress that would certify two-year medical schools. If more citizens can afford a medical education, the result will be more doctors, lower prices for health care and less reliance on health-care plans. As one medical student at the University of Guam explains, "We're all built the same. If you can't figure out where someone's heart is without taking a course, you're *really* in trouble."

We're also offering a series of inexpensive "how-to" brochures to public schools. Students from fifth through twelfth grade can learn surgery, dermatology (a perennial student concern) and obstetrics right in the classroom. We hope that this program will one day become as popular as driver's education—and perhaps that day is not so far off, as many driver's-ed teachers are being asked to teach medicine as well.

Other Domestic Affairs

☐ UNIONS. To keep unions from being so self-centered, the Government is formally changing the common names of many occupations. Thus the official title for "plumber" is now "toilet man." Chefs will be known as "fatmakers," teachers as "bossy showoffs," miners as "muddies" and steelworkers as "ores."

☐ WORKERS COMPENSATION PROGRAMS. Workers with diseases caused by

As of October 31, 1984, your Social Security card will become a handy charge plate. You'll be able to charge gourmet meals, elegant clothes, airline tickets and cat food by the case. The monthly total will be deducted from your Social Security payment. It's the new way to buy the luxuries you require—without having to cash your Social Security checks.

asbestos will be transferred to firefighting programs, where their natural fireproofing will be a great advantage.

☐ IMMIGRATION. As of 1985, the only aliens permitted entrance to the United States will be the winners of national pageants held in their home countries. These pageants, known as "Mr. USA," "Mrs. USA," "Miss USA" and "Baby USA," will judge candidates on appearance, tractability, motivation and Christianness. Runners-up will receive $200 scholarships to the American university of their choice.

☐ HAITIAN REFUGEES. To alleviate American guilt about the way Haitian refugees are treated, they have been officially declared Poison Pig People (PPP).

☐ SCHOOL BILINGUALISM. It is ethnocentric to assume that all schoolchildren should speak English, and it is anthropocentric to assume that all students should be human beings.

☐ AIR TRAFFIC CONTROLLERS. The President is going to fire all the new air traffic controllers in addition to the ones he's already fired. He wants to make sure none of them get the chance to walk out on the American people again.

☐ WOMEN. Women have had a very nice coin with Susan B. Anthony on it issued in their honor, and they rejected it. We cannot constantly be knocking ourselves out thinking of new ways to keep them happy.

Special Presidential Assistant Anita Bryant gets the credit for legislation requiring all women to devote one day out of each work week to volunteer service. Those with jobs must work Saturdays and Sundays.

THE DEPARTMENT OF THE INTERIOR:

It's a little frightening, running the Department of the Interior. There's just so *much* of America to keep an eye on. Wild animals to track...valuable minerals to strip-mine... offshore waters to drill in...Indian reservations to guard. We're willing to bet that even the Founding Fathers didn't want Squanto or a pack of timber wolves moving in! And neither do we.

You see, it's our job to protect you from an environment that can become—well—a little excessive at times. That's why we've been wondering lately just what's so priceless about our "priceless natural resources." Frankly, we think that "priceless" is just a fancy word for "not for sale." We've proved that by auctioning off millions of acres of Government land that were once deemed unmarketable by the bird-watching naysayers of the granola crowd.

It's time to think about what the Department of the Interior should be. Time to think about where we're going and where we will have been when we look at today tomorrow.

Time to think about what's most important for all of us.

Query 1984: What is Beauty?

Over the past four years, the Department of the Interior has been a department of "re's." There's *re*storation and *re*forestation and *re*paration and *re*llenos, those chilis we're so fond of. But the most important "re" is "*re*definition." (And let's talk right now about redefining "acid" rain. Acid is *not* the poison people seem to think it is. DNA is an acid. So is RNA. And these acids, scientists say, are the building blocks of the universe.)

One of the Department's major tasks in the past four years has been to redefine what is beautiful. In the prodigal Administrations of the past, "beauty" seems to have been equated with "massive expense." Certainly the Grand Canyon is worth seeing—but it represents the kind of make-work project our Government can no longer afford. It would take even the finest American craftsmen

Outdoorsmen have flocked to the new Hooker Chemical National Park, an attractive recreation area with enough holding ponds to accommodate tons of surplus residue. Part of the thrill is the exciting challenge posed by the park's rugged environment. Here, one hearty naturalist enjoys the therapeutic powers of pesticide silt. As Park Ranger Herman Cudahy remarked: "Dumping—by all means; dunking— perhaps not." What a place to park!

A Time to Redefine

years—at an appalling cost—to build a structure like that today. Besides, how many Americans can ever afford the chance to visit the Grand Canyon? Isn't it more important to create beauty in ordinary spots, places the average citizen doesn't have to spend a fortune to visit?

We've brought nature to more Americans than ever before with our Buns 'n Beauty Program—our three-year effort to upgrade the salad bars in America's restaurants. How many people have ever noticed what a lovely piece of nature a salad bar is? It's the whole of America's natural bounty, all lined up: crisp greens with their springtime freshness, mellow fruits and vegetables reminiscent of the harvest, golden croutons scattered like bits of driftwood on a beach. With our help, salad bars will be able to offer other views of nature as well...wildflowers, icicles, minnows. In this way, hundreds of thousands of citizens can appreciate nature along with their hamburgers.

Of course, we can't deal only with small jobs. Sometimes we have to think *big*. Last year we embarked on one of the most ambitious beautification campaigns in the Interior's history: the Scenic Billboard Highway Program.

For this program, thousands of billboards painted with inspirational scenes from nature have been strategically placed along the nation's highways wherever they'll do the most good. (In urban areas, the billboards are scented as well.) It's an attractive and inexpensive way to beautify the landscape, and drivers are as enthusiastic as environmentalists. "I used to hate the sight of Syracuse," confesses one commuter. "But now there are these gorgeous underwater scenes along the road, so I don't have to see it at all. It's like being in a Cousteau show!" The real beauty of it all is that our push to "sign up" America has actually turned into a profit-making venture, thanks to the huge demand for advertising space on the backs of all our new billboards!

And we've made significant improvements in our national parks. In response to

Leopard, ocelot, Kodiak bear—the choice is yours in the Pelt Room at the Endangered Species Hall of Fame. Here the most jaded shopper will find something "just right" and learn more about the environment as well. "Before I came here I felt guilty about wanting a Bengal tiger hand warmer," reported a satisfied customer. "Now I have one."

Few regret the passing of the whooping crane. Though beautiful, it is one of the noisiest living things in the world. Our laboratory-bred birds, on the other hand, live forever, can be used in a variety of ways and never "make whoopie."

It seems, oh, only about a half-hour ago that my father handed me my first gun and told me, 'Neil, get outside and shoot those squirrels on the roof.' He must have gotten me mixed up with my brother. You know, my father was a very good man in many ways, but he did have that struggle with alcohol, and I guess his aim wasn't what it could have been. So I went out there and gosh, when I saw how nice it was outside, and how cute and bushy those squirrels were playing around up there...well, I've just enjoyed hunting and the outdoors ever since.

You know, people think I don't care about the environment. But that's just not true. I think my ranch is the nicest spot on earth. 'God's hundreds of little acres,' I call it. Out there I feel free to ride, or sweep the porch, or—I'm not afraid to say it—just get down on my knees and pray a little.

It's not all a bed of roses, of course. Once when I was riding around, I saw a snake. Well, golly, I just burst out crying—I thought it was a cobra. But then one of my Secret Service men came up and said it wasn't poisonous. Still, Nancy and I never walked around barefoot after that!

Sometimes I wish that all Americans, whatever their nationality, could own a ranch like mine. But of course, one of the things that makes my ranch so nice is that not too many people have one like it. It's a problem. Maybe one of these days Tip O'Neill will figure it out for me!

consumer demand, our researchers discovered that environmentalists wanted their nature tougher, more "natural." We've complied.

For example, we've *re*routed the entrance road to Hot Springs National Park. Arriving campers never know now when they'll find themselves shot 20 feet into the air by a fightin' mad geyser. Surprise mud baths dot the Devil's Bathtub campgrounds: Take a step in the middle of the night and you never know where you'll end up! And animal lovers will finally have a chance to really be one with the animals they're trying so hard to protect: By the spring of 1985, hunters will be allowed full range through the national park. We can't guarantee they'll always shoot straight—but that's part of the fun.

Wild Kingdom for the Eighties

Whatever environmentalists may say, the simple fact is that there are so many animals in this country that it's impossible to keep track of them all. Not even a department the size of ours has the time or manpower to make sure that every single species is still there! How much more efficient, then, to put our primary emphasis on the species we know are abundant—what we call the Very Important Species—and to devote ourselves to protecting *them*.

Saving vanishing species means you have to give them a place to live. For every yellow-bellied sapsucker we save, countless potential jobs could be lost: These birds build their nests *right* where a new block of condos was going to go up.

For every household pet we save, on the other hand, *no jobs are lost*. Perhaps the pet is even a poodle whose elegant coat requires frequent clipping: Another dog salon opens, and unemployment goes down a tenth of a percent. That's why we think it's important to get our priorities in order.

Of course, not all endangered species deprive workers of jobs. Some are just plain objectionable. That's why we've stripped them of their "privileged" status.

Update:
The Endangered Species List

Removed	Reason
Snail Darter	Too small and "darty"
Black-footed Ferret	Member of weasel family
Silson's Antelope	Has poisonous antlers
Short-tailed Hawk	Scares small, cute mammals
Gray Mole	Rolls own feces into ball
House Sparrow	Extremely common
Praying Mantis	Is an insect

What we're talking about here is survival of the fittest—the very notion our harshest critics are always trying to jam down the throats of schoolchildren. But that includes moral fitness, too. The way we see it, Darwin can't have meant that sly, mean animals, like foxes, have the right to claw their way to the top! We think we owe it to America to see that *only* the fittest survive.

And we're not sleeping on the job! True, there may be only a few individuals left in the species that *are* worth protecting. But we believe that what's important is quality, not quantity. Each member of these species receives unparalleled care. There are just

The least important—but most colorful—branch of the Department of the Interior is the Bureau of Indian Affairs. America's first inhabitants, these proud and attractive people command our sincere respect with their superb craftsmanship and their many feats of derring-do. We know they are too "Indy-pendent" to want our help, so we offer them a hearty handshake instead. Men of the undergrowth, America salutes you!

four whooping cranes left...and each of them has been custom-fitted with mink wingwarmers. It's little touches like that that make all the difference.

WE, THE PEOPLE #1

I'm only three days old, and already life is so exciting! Now that hunters are allowed in the park, they'll really keep me on the go. You could say I learned how to run before I learned how to walk. They got my mother yesterday, right between the eyes with a crossbow. Left a clean exit wound. I saw her being carried out on a station wagon. It's hard, but I know it'll end up being for the better—I really have to learn how to take care of myself and be independent.

Justice
A Time to Pry, a Time to Fry

Justice. It's a heavyweight concept, all right. One of those highfalutin words that big-shot lawyers and pointy-headed professors love to toss around to show they're better than you. But what's justice really all about? What's it mean to the little guy? Here at USCO, we have a good idea. Justice? It's just this: Rights. You have 'em. We have 'em.

Anybody tries to take away your rights, don't worry, the boys down at Justice are gonna blow him away faster than he can yell "Get me the ACLU!" And that's why it's called Justice. It's not for them. Just us.

Susie Cass, seven, discovers the joy of praying to the Lord. A national task force of Federal judges is now enforcing the Voluntary School Prayer Amendment, aided by our effective Child Informant Network.

Full-Court Press

We're not just making justice more just, we're making it fast. In today's stress-wracked, wacko-paced world, we know you want your justice in a hurry. You can't afford to wait around for the legal niceties that reflect the leisurely pace of an earlier time. That's why we've developed a convenient new justice concept to unclog our constipated court system—Lawmobiles. These court-houses on wheels (actually Toyota pickups with a judge's bench mounted in back) prowl our urban combat zones. Dispatched to crime scenes by police radio, they try arrested criminals on the spot. At once, the old reliable bail system is rendered obsolete and all witnesses are right there when you need them. Each vehicle carries a judge/driver and a paralegal who acts as both prosecutor and defense counsel. If a defendant is convicted, the Lawmobile immediately delivers him to prison or—in capital punishment cases—economically carries out the sentence by tossing him out the back as it speeds through traffic to its next case.

Breakup of the Supremes

We're also working to boost efficiency at our overburdened Supreme Court. Last year, the caseload was so heavy that Chief Justice Warren Burger had to suspend his own policy of allowing justices to do piecework between cases, despite Justice William Rehnquist's bitter complaints that he would lose

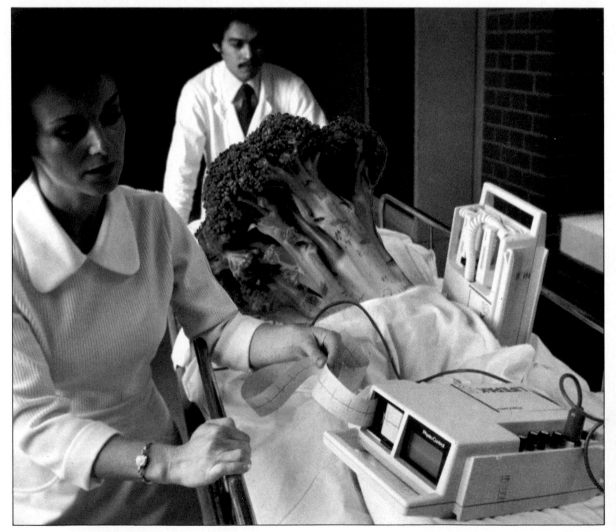

Dedicated medical professionals struggle to preserve the life of a *brassica oleracea italica*, better known as Baby Green Giant. A cruel Long Island couple was caught in the act of steaming this unique life form when FBI agents raided their home.

thousands of dollars performing wedding ceremonies on the steps of the Supreme Court Building.

The biggest efficiency killer, though, is the age of the justices, now averaging 93.7 years, and the inability of many of them to hear arguments due to deafness or senility. After a medical study showed that more than half the Court would probably expire within the next half hour, the President designated nine new justice nominees who could step in as soon as a present justice is nullified—in mid-case, if necessary. The new justices are already on the job in the Supreme Court basement, hearing less important cases to further reduce the case load. The designates are Phyllis Schlafly, Jerry Falwell, Oral Roberts, Billy Graham, Roy Cohn, William Clark, Anita Bryant, Billy Martin and the nation's most respected jurist, Judge Joseph Wapner of the popular *People's Court*.

F(or) B(igger) I(ncome)

The FBI has long been one of America's most beloved institutions, on a par with Yellowstone National Park, Disneyland and *Family Feud*. But the FBI has always had one weakness: It never made a profit.

At USCO, we're working to change that. First, we pulled our agents off the wasteful, unnecessary pursuit of so-called white-collar criminals—a totally mythological species. These agents were put to much better use. We've rented them out to act as celebrity bodyguards and security guards at shopping malls, ball parks, rock concerts and other legitimate business concerns. Any agents not rented are assigned to track down the predatory blue-collar criminals who commit industrial pilferage and who shoplift at K-Mart and 7-11, costing our economy untold billions.

In another problem area, the Bureau has resumed its popular entrapment program to root out crime in one of America's most dangerous and lawless environments— Congress. This year's ABSCAM target: the many Senators and Representatives who fit the psychological profile of potential serial murderers. A dozen FBI agents ingeniously disguised as teenage beauty queens have begun dating these legislators and attempting to provoke attack by withholding sex, ques-

The aging Justices of the Supreme Court bring a seasoned measure of experience to all their major decisions. And the Administration is doing everything possible to make their lives easier, including making advance arrangements for all the Court's transportation needs.

tioning their manhood and similar "tease" tactics. Any solons who respond violently will be arrested and charged with assault, murder and unlawfully attempting intercourse with a Federal officer in drag.

Lording It Over Us

Guess who's back and bigger than ever? Yes, it's good old God himself! Not even all the atheists, liberals, evolutionists and union leaders in America could keep the Deity down for long.

First came that overdue Supreme Court decision allowing municipal governments to bring you Nativity scenes at Christmastime. In its major initiative for the year, our Civil Rights Division, belying criticism from radicals that it no longer protects minority rights, ordered that all such Nativities be integrated. The panel decreed that at least one out of every three Wise Men or shepherd figures attending the Christ Child must be recognizably black, Hispanic, Oriental or homosexual.

The much-needed School Prayer Amendment will most likely pass this year, and we're already planning our enforcement strategy. It's one thing to write a law, but quite another to make the little urchins pray. We're also recommending passage of the controversial Womb Prayer Amendment. Why? Because the right of the unborn to pray must also be guaranteed. Under it, expectant moms must attend regular church services so their developing offspring may worship. After all, fetuses have spiritual needs, too.

It seems to me that our system of justice has gotten pretty far away from what the good Lord intended. We've gotten too complicated. Too caught up in what I like to call 'legalities.'

Let me give you an example: When I was appointed President, there were a lot of guys I wanted to hire on and appoint and such, to get on with the business of running this country. Well let me tell you what I spent the first two or three months of my Administration doing—sorting out all the legal wrangling and the hairy eyeballs Congress and the press gave my friends.

These men are willing to devote four years of service to their country. I don't see where we get off making them account for who they sold their house to and things like that.

I remember some of my friends were reduced to tears by the kind of harassment they got. Do we need a system of justice like that? No way! These men have jobs to do— and they're not doing them for the money either. Most of these guys earn more money parting their hair than they will in four years of Government service.

That's the kind of stuff I'm talking about when I say we need a less complicated system of justice.

Life Is Just a Bowl of Fungus

Which brings us to the famed "Baby Jane Doe Case," in which your Justice Department moved forcefully to protect a postbirth baby born with defects so severe as to render it indistinguishable from broccoli. Following that, the Department pursued the equally important "Mother and Father Doe Case," opposing the attempt of Baby Jane's parents to commit suicide after they got a look at the medical bills from Baby Jane's doctors.

In the much publicized "Baby Oscar Mayer Case," a couple from Pennsylvania was prosecuted when they attempted to destroy an unidentifiable life form which had incubated for six months in the back of their refrigerator. Lawyers for the couple argued that the victim, believed to have begun life as presliced bologna, could at best be classified a higher form of mold. But expert medical witnesses testified for the prosecution that if preserved, the youngster might be able to lead a full, rich life, though it would probably always have an irrational dread of mustard.

Uncle Sam and Auntie Trust

Our Antitrust Division (or Auntie, as we like to call it) has had an exciting year full of controversy and wild office parties. First, Auntie sued the nation's newly separated telephone companies, demanding that they return to being the one gigantic, cantankerous but familiar monopoly we all knew and loved. Because, as Auntie lawyers argued in their closely reasoned legal brief to the Supreme Court, "this mess we've got now just plain *ain't working*." Furthermore, the brief held, touching a note virtually all Americans agree with, "We miss ole Ma Bell."

Then, in an even more daring step, the Antitrust Division sued *itself* and demanded its own dissolution, contending that most of its actions over the years had been "inimical to the health of private enterprise and pretty darn annoying besides." The unit then renamed itself the Antirust Division and pledged to fight for the preservation of gleaming metal finishes in America's tools, vehicles and household products.

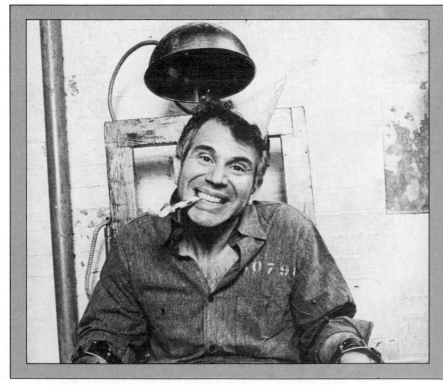

WE, THE PEOPLE #2

When a man comes up to you in the darkness and he is clutching the glistening knife to your throat or the gun he purchased because it *was* his constitutional right to bear those arms and he has *his* arms around your windpipe you must strike back with your being, with your manhood, and draw the first blood, the blood of all being the sweet, red blood of death that will drain from the mother who will take your life just as *we* the convicts will suck the life from you if we get out of this hole the prison that you Mr. America have placed us in or is it you Mr. America who is on the inside saving yourself from us who wait for...
pain of the bullets
...from the Mormon guns...
ripping our flesh
and you better thank god as we thank god for this death at the end of the death row because USCO is making the system work again.

The Economy
Everyone's a Winner!

In the old days, people were mainly attracted to such occupations as priest or cowboy. Then it became fashionable to be an intrusive Government bureaucrat. Now the vogue has shifted once more: Everyone wants to be in business.

No wonder. We have made it *exciting*. For Americans who are corporations, our Administration has practically eliminated income taxes. The emerging service sector is growing at a remarkable clip, and everyone from stock brokers to domestic servants is benefiting. Nor have we neglected the old "smokestack" industries that have made America prosperous and tough and, in a good way, sort of smelly. Factories are being retooled to handle our emergency military buildup, while industrial robots are teaching workers a thing or two about good work habits and "fair" labor contracts.

The country went off in search of excellence, and found us. Old Uncle Sam has got himself a well-cut gray suit at last. He has straightened his tie, shined his shoes, touched up his hair. He's traveling first-class. He is making a bundle. And that makes us proud.

The U.S. economy's expanding service sector need not displace traditional industrial processes or employees thanks to generous tax credits now allowed large companies that do not want to pay taxes. Here, former auto workers on the assembly line at Pillsbury's newly opened Burger King Plant No. 3 have been retrained to fill jobs in the growth field of the 1980s. "I hear the Japanese have nothing to compare with this," crows Special Sauce Applicator Vern Cruikshank (left).

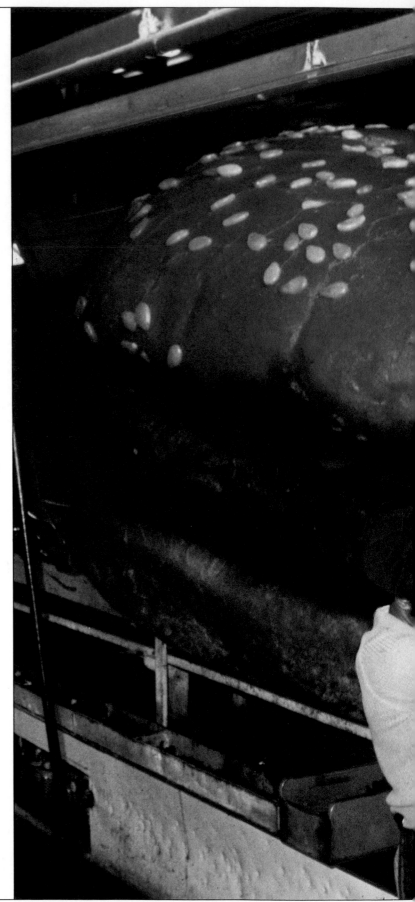

Raymond Donovan still heads the Department of Labor, despite the popular misconception that he resigned in disgrace.

The Reagan Economic Miracle

Americans knew their economy was in bad shape in 1981. Few citizens, however, understood just how feeble, how ravaged the U.S. economy had become before we took control.

Everyone remembers that inflation had hit 37 percent annually under the previous Administration and that the prime interest rate was inching toward 50 percent. Most people recall that in December 1980 fully half of all blue-collar workers were unemployed, terminally ill or suffering from hallucinations brought on by the Democrats' overregulation of industry.

Those were grim days indeed. But few Americans realize that during the late 1970s, the U.S. Treasury had been forced to pawn most of its gold reserves in order to subsidize New York City's costly system of free gourmet food and kitchen appliances for the poor. Nor did the general public have any idea that the Carter Administration, in an effort intended to make U.S. industry more competitive, had drawn up legislation that required automakers to manufacture cars in only two colors—gray and brown. The Social Security system? To cut expenses and forestall bankruptcy during the last few months of 1980, the system's administrators began sending out play money and worthless sweepstake entries to the visually disabled and retirees over 80.

We have changed all that (except for the sweepstake entries). Inflation is down to less than 5 percent. Interest rates, now at just 12 percent, have fallen low enough so that almost every American family could afford a new speedboat *and* a trip to Oberammergau last summer. Everyone not too lazy to work has a job, and a job he or she likes—often in the booming computer industry, which the Reagan Administration started, sort of. People are inviting friends over for money-counting parties; workers and managers are square-dancing together after hours in clean, humming factories. Economic life is worth living again.

As part of our new Public Relations Zone Program, decaying industrial cities have been transformed into promising urban frontiers where the can-do spirit is keen. In Indiana, the once dreary, woebegone city of Gary, now rechristened Pleasantville, is experiencing a renaissance of self-esteem.

What's So New About New Ideas?

During the endless media circus fight over who should be this year's Democratic Presidential candidate and sacrificial lamb, there was a lot of talk about "new ideas"—and one of those ideas was something called "industrial policy." But such a policy, devoted to making American workers *work* again and American industry *indust* once more, is nothing new. Indeed, the Reagan Administration launched its own successful industrial policy almost as soon as the President took office. Corporations were granted statehood and the right to maintain standing armies. Many workers received extended vacation time; some even experienced the thrill of the great outdoors as tenting under the stars became the latest national craze. And businessmen responded with enthusiasm and responsibility to the Administration's calls for voluntary industry self-regulation.

Much of the Administration's industrial policy has been little noticed or ignored by the press. For instance, the bosses of orga-nized labor have incessantly publicized their plan for dangerous, job-hogging protectionism in the form of domestic content legislation—a measure now pending in Congress to require that every imported automobile contain a certain fraction of American-made parts. The President, however, contending that U.S. consumers would end up paying higher prices, has proposed his own 1984 Auto Import Act. The measure—a "new idea" if there ever was one—would merely require that foreign carmakers install exploding gas tanks, faulty disc brakes and automatic transmissions that shift into reverse under certain atmospheric conditions, thus wiping out any unfair competitive advantages.

The Commerce Department has also established an Executive Advisory Team to help keep the reinvigorated economy on track. Although the several hundred team members, who call themselves "the Piece-of-the-Action Corps," are all former top executives, each has pledged to charge the

Latissue Johnson, 17, still practices her unfortunate trade in downtown St. Louis, but her Public Relations Zone case worker has provided an attractive outfit and Government-issue breath mints.

Under previous spendthrift Administrations, the United States Postal Service issued dozens of commemoratives each year. The stamps tended to honor everyone from foreigners to 17th-century atheists, but they neglected regular, popular Americans and their achievements. Our money-saving 1985 Commemorative Postal Series will consist of just six stamps that will delight collectors and at the same time save taxpayers millions.

Arthur Laffer helped make this country rich again by taking the dismal and the science out of the dismal science.

Edward Teller helped to give his country one of its greatest gifts—the means to prevent nuclear war by waging it.

Wayne Newton is not just a man, but a way of life.

Vic Morrow gave his life heroically defending his country—and his industry.

America's most physically fit President ever!

In less than half a century, Palm Springs has become emblematic of America itself: sunny, well-swept, neat, air conditioned.

A significant portion of the Reagan economic program has been fashioned by ordinary Americans at Saturday afternoon "think tanks" all over the country. The St. Petersburg, Florida, Rotary Club is responsible for an intriguing plan to wipe out the national debt by having U.S. mail carriers sell 450 billion pecan-studded jumbo chocolate bars door to door.

Government a consulting fee of no more than $1,200 per day. From their headquarters in Palos Verdes Estates, California, they are assigned to assist small, floundering companies around the country. Team member Harrumpher ("Pete") Kiernan, retired General Manager of United Technologies's Anti-Personnel Division, speaks fondly of the two weeks he spent teaching a Seattle clothing company the basics of management. Recalls Kiernan: "They dress like pansies up there. So I said, 'Get a decent suit! And don't drink herb tea at the office!' They also made their product out of silk, for God's sake, and had the damn things sewn together there in Seattle. 'What—you've never heard of rayon?' I asked them. 'Singapore—forty cents per worker per day!' I said. 'You're supposed to be running a *business* here!' I told them. I think it was damn useful for that outfit to have me around."

Slicker Cities

America's cities have been in decline for too long, and the failed policies of the past have only hastened urban decay. Crime is as bad as everyone says—worse, even. City streets are pocked, threatening the suspensions of even large, smooth-riding luxury cars. Mass transit systems have become tawdry at best, filled with non-white youths between 16 and 21 at worst. The urban middle class has fled to the suburbs to live with responsible people in a decent environment

—and to send their children to schools where extra credit is not awarded for having abortions.

The Commerce Department has launched a massive, nine-month $45,000 program to make our cities *nice* again. We will achieve our restoration of urban America not with expensive social engineering or vast pork-barrel giveaways to corrupt city hall bureaucrats. Rather, our Hello City program is based on plain, hard, proven principles—good old-fashioned public relations. We are out to convince Americans that the degenerative disease of the cities has been cured, that the old, shabby cities of the East and the Midwest are delightful, vital places. If we can tap the power of positive, optimistic thinking and somehow direct it like a laser beam at those horrible cities, then urban dwellers and traditional Americans alike will be in a better mood to move on and tackle other tough national challenges.

We will carry out the Hello City program in three stages. During Phase I, beginning this winter, nine urban areas will be designated U.S. Public Relations Zones. Within the boundaries of each PRZ, normal truth-in-advertising standards will be suspended, so that Cleveland, for example, would be free to claim that it has an average of 317 sunny days per year, that its violent-crime rate is the lowest in the U.S. and that all of its city parks contain buried treasure.

Phase II will consist primarily of a unique incentive program designed to encourage urban residents to make their cities more congenial places, especially for visitors. In return for standing up straight and shouting "Go for it, America!" several times daily, eligible PRZ dwellers will be allotted full quotas of antibiotics, salt and electric power.

Phase III will be the most ambitiously unorthodox of all and will require an infusion of private-sector monies. Phase III projects might include sensible public housing designs, such as the Federally funded prototype recently built by the Schiavone Construction Co. in Newark, N.J., and small-

You know, I have watched a lot of administrations come and go over the last 50 years—some from our party, some from the opposition party...although none, so far as I know, from any other party, a 'third party' it's called, because, well, we in the American form of Government have always pretty much been committed to a two-party form of Government. Which as my old friend Fred Allen said about one of his wives I think it was, 'She may be a stinker but by golly she's my very own stinker!'

But we've had the administrations come and go, and the most successful ones, the politically successful ones, I've always noticed, have had a good slogan, a catchy name that the people remember and like. Now, some of our opponents have put that 'Reaganomics' tag on our program for economic recovery. 'Reaganomics' was not our name—that was a critical, negative thing...as Jack Warner once said to me in the 1940s or '50s when they were dismantling what they called 'the studio system,' Jack Warner said, 'Ron, you know, I'll bet if we called it "the good old movie gang" instead of "the studio system," we wouldn't have Washington on our backs now!' And that's the same thing, in principle, we have here now with tags that critics have put on our economic program.

It's time that we put our own good title, I guess you could call it, to our Administration's policy. Franklin D. Roosevelt, of course, had the New Deal. Harry S. Truman modified that, now, and had his Fair Deal. We are calling our program—the tax cuts and the fat-cutting and, well, prosperity—we're calling it the Highly Profitable Deal. Because every American ought to be able to make a good profit, and with God's help we're trying to make that dream a reality.

Where have all the Negroes gone? On Manhattan's Lower East Side, the census taker assigned to the borough conducts our revised 1984 population survey. Interestingly, preliminary indications are that fewer than 5,000 black people live in New York City.

scale mass transit programs such as the Limo-Link pilot project now undergoing testing and development using Government limousines in downtown Washington. In Boston, Federal seed money has underwritten an experimental Phase III project whereby prostitutes are provided free medical care by visiting Japanese—many of them physicians—in return for wearing modest, Government-issue street attire.

Furthermore, each PRZ city will be renamed, given a peppy new municipal slogan and provided with an appealing civic logo.

U.S. Public Relations Zones
A New Start for American Cities

Detroit . . . . . . becomes. . . .	**Mt. Carmel**—"The Thanksgiving City"	
Pittsburgh . . . . . becomes. . . .	**Sweet Grass**—"Birthplace of Beethoven and Einstein"	
St. Louis . . . . . becomes. . . .	**Stronghurst**—"The Playground Metropolis"	
Scranton . . . . . becomes. . . .	**Arroyo Grande**—"Summer Wonderland"	
Yonkers . . . . . becomes. . . .	**Hot Springs**—"America's Avignon"	
Baltimore . . . . . becomes. . . .	**Oakwood**—"City of Forests"	
Buffalo . . . . . . becomes. . . .	**Emerald Bay**—"Plenty of Everything for Everyone"	
Cleveland . . . . . becomes. . . .	**Newport**—"Sun and Fun Town"	
Gary, Ind. . . . . . becomes. . . .	**Pleasantville**—"A New Concept in Urban Family Living"	

WE, THE PEOPLE #3

You try juggling a husband, a child, a semiprofessional squash career, the Junior League *and* a full-time business.

I manufacture sequined intrauterine devices for sale overseas. I started the business. I run it. When we opened in 1977, we almost closed—this simply insufferable Occupational Safety and Health Administration inspector told me I had to provide special asbestos uniforms for all my people who worked near the kilns. But that wasn't all: The Labor Department said I had to contribute to Social Security—even though two-thirds of them are illegals. When the National Labor Relations Board ruled that I could not fire the little monkeys for refusing to help out at my League luncheons, I very nearly gave up, I really did.

Thank you, President Reagan. Thank you for those nice new (and *funny*) fellows who do the OSHA inspections. Thank you for making people other than corporations pay their share of income taxes for a change. Thank you, Mr. President, for letting this modern woman achieve equal rights *her* own way.

The President and Madame Reagan
Request the Honour of Your Presence
At Their Quadrennial Inauguration Gala
Monday the Twenty-First of January
Beginning at
Half Past Seven O'Clock in the Evening
Alfred Bloomingdale Rotunda
The Hall of Magnificence
(Formerly the Department of Education)
Four Hundred Maryland Avenue,
Southwest Washington,
District of Columbia,
United States of America

G.O.P. Amulets

White Tie

We're already making plans for a fabulous second-term Inaugural Celebration. We'll spare no expense in making this the most exciting party ever. What better way could there be to mark the start of what promises to be a gala-packed four years? See you there!

January 21, 1985

Schedule of Events

Noon	Benediction by the Reverend Jerry Falwell. Flyover of F/A-18 Hornet jet fighter squadron with indiscriminate ceremonial firing of Sidewinder missles
12:15 p.m.	Oath of Office administered by Supreme Court Chief Justice-designee William Clark
12:30 p.m.	Inaugural procession along Pennsylvania Avenue. President and Mme. Reagan toss commemorative coins to crowd from new Presidential dirigible
1:15 p.m.	Ed Meese Defense Fund Benefit Luncheon. Smithsonian: Cabinet officers model new uniforms and departmental crowns
2:45 p.m.	Naptime
5:30 p.m.	Rose Garden, The White House: Mme. Reagan presides over ceremony legally designating the West Highland white terrier the national pet
7:30 p.m.	Inaugural Gala, Hall of Magnificence: Entertainment by Shamu the Killer Whale and the Dallas Cowboy Cheerleaders; catering by Buckets o' Truffles
11:30 p.m.	Hoover Room, The White House: Surprise announcement by the President

Visions of Inaugural splendour (clockwise from above): It takes a mighty wide screen to give the Great Communicator a comfortable fit; the stunning Bechtel Pavillion (formerly the Kennedy Center); mushroom-cloud fireworks brighten the night sky; George Shultz thrills the gathered masses with his rocket-powered sedan chair; antique White House guard uniforms add an air of dignity.

Foreign Policy
Very Diplomatic Affairs

America the weak. America the defensive. America the shamed. America the spat upon and laughed at by Communist tyrants and Third World terrorists whom we could squash just like *that* if we felt like it. Such was America's pitiable reputation around the world when the Reagan Administration took control of your overseas operations.

No more. Nowadays, animals howl when American ambassadors arrive. Foreign leaders visibly quake as they open mail from the U.S. Government. Little countries request our permission for everything—just recently, for instance, Costa Rica asked for Washington's okay to change the design of its currency. (Approval denied.) Communist dictators are beginning to admit, in private, when they are drunk, that America is the best country on earth. The first four letters of President Reagan are the first four letters of "prestige." Libya spelled backwards is alibi, and you know what that means.

Grenada? Ours. Nicaragua? Just wait and see. Lebanon? Bold initiatives are under way. In short, the world is our Osterizer. America is on top again.

Last spring in Beirut, shrewd American negotiators surprised fractious Lebanese leaders with a surprise display of Washington's sincerity and diplomatic sophistication. After performing her interpretive dance depicting reconciliation between Sunni Moslem and Maronite Christian factions, Deputy Assistant Secretary of State Brenda Connelly received well-earned praise from the Secretary and from the Lebanese sultans.

This lucky recipient of tasty soybean oil got 300 trading stamps as an added bonus. All she needs is 300 more and she can get a 50 mm. machine gun.

In the Oval Office, the President discusses an historic new quinine export agreement with a key political leader or civil servant or high priest of Indonesia—surprisingly, the fifth most populous country in the world.

An Overnight Sensation

It did not take weeks or months for the Reagan Administration to achieve an historic foreign policy success. It took less than an hour. Just 41 minutes after the President became the President, he had forced the Iranians to surrender—and free the 52 Americans held hostage in Teheran. What was President Reagan's secret? Nothing but good old Yankee toughness and a funny kind of godlike omniscience, as well as a firm determination that *every* hostage be sent home, regardless of race, creed or sex. Under the previous Administration, the few hostages who had been released were women or blacks. Such Carter-era "affirmative action" may have pleased the Democrats' friends in the Third World, but it was cold comfort to those left behind in their Iranian gulag for 444 days.

After that spectacular start, it was inevitable that in other areas Reagan diplomacy would have to succeed more slowly. Of course, there have been many stunning achievements in foreign affairs—all the ones that everybody knows about. And there have also been a few disappointments. South African leaders have not yet responded to the U.S. Government Candygram, sent in 1981 or 1982 along with a message suggesting that most black people do deserve the right to vote. And despite almost four years of U.S. pressure, Russia is still a totalitarian Communist state. Yet our analysts believe that all

of these setbacks have the same basic source —*the stubborn refusal of foreign countries to agree with America*. Only when our adversaries abroad accept that fundamental principle can a meaningful dialogue begin.

Some of our critics have attempted to make a partisan issue out of America's efforts to avoid nuclear war. That is wrong. For, like all Americans, white and black, rich and poor, good and bad, we in the Reagan Administration would like to avoid the nightmare of a nuclear holocaust *if at all possible*. Should that ideal prove unattainable, our backup plan would be to avoid losing any nuclear war. This is not the same as seeking to "win" such a war, since we all know that there are no winners in a nuclear war. Also, nuclear war is unthinkable. So don't think about it.

Arms Control and Dutch Treaties

Critics have claimed that our Administration has not pursued arms control negotiations eagerly enough. Yet we seek only peace. After all, it was not we who walked away from the bargaining tables in Geneva last year. It was the Soviets. It was not we who dismissed the "zero option," a proposal for eliminating nuclear warheads from Europe. That too was the Soviets. It is not we who are deploying new Pershing II and cruise missiles in Western Europe—no, wait. Okay. That *is* us. And, okay, we have refused Soviet overtures about negotiating a ban on antisatellite weapons in space. But they're probably not really serious about it anyway, and even if they would sign some kind of treaty, they'd almost be sure to break it someday. And experts remind us about the problems of verification. Can America be everywhere all at once to make sure that all arms control treaties are observed? Of course not—only God has that power. And it is no coincidence that our Soviet adversaries claim that God does not exist.

Still, we are attempting to negotiate in good faith. The Reagan Administration will go anywhere at any time to meet with anyone about anything. Then we will come home.

One sign of our seriousness: Beginning on January 1, Michael Korda (author of *Strategic Superiority: How to Get It, How to Use It!*) will become Director of the U.S. Arms Control and Disarmament Agency. Indeed, Director-designate Korda has already improved U.S. negotiating posture vis-à-vis the Soviets. For instance, at a diplomatic reception in Washington last summer, to most observers Korda seemed to greet Soviet Ambassador Anatoly Dobrynin in an ordinary way. However, Korda first gripped the Russian's hand with unusual force, then planted his right foot between Dobrynin's feet. As the men chatted, Korda stared intently at the ambassador's neck. Later, when he offered to freshen Dobrynin's drink, the savvy American negotiator instead simply walked off to spend the rest of the evening in conversation with a low-level South Korean cultural attaché. By all accounts, the Soviet emissary was unnerved—and Korda says that as a result, he expects Moscow to accept a forthcoming new U.S. arms control plan.

The particulars of that draft treaty, of course, are still secret, and so technical that nobody really understands them anyway. But some of the basic points include a requirement that Moscow permit American manufacturers to compete for Soviet nuclear weapons contracts; that when any international crisis threatens to escalate into a nuclear exchange, both sides will refrain from crossed fingers and double dares; that in the event of conventional war in Central Europe, Moscow and Washington will confer to determine if they *really* care all *that* much about the fate of the West or East Germans; and that Santa Barbara, California, be designated a "nuclear-free" zone.

The public figure, the private man: In a rare picture of President Reagan's desk top aboard Air Force One, White House photographer David Hume Cravenly captured a telling glimpse of the tools and talismans that comprise the Commander-in-Chief's very special world.

Yet control of nuclear arms is not the only realm of diplomacy and negotiations. Indeed, the Reagan Administration has a sheaf of signed-and-sealed foreign policy achievements. Perhaps the most significant:

☐ A pioneering accord with Indonesia governing the export of quinine by-products. Failure to achieve this treaty might possibly have resulted in full-scale civil war in Indonesia.

☐ A ground-breaking agreement with Italy calling for the educational exchange of civil defense officials.

☐ An extraordinary series of treaties with Nepal declaring 1986 the International Year of Nepalese Hides and naming Pokhara the sister city of Elko, Nevada.

☐ An epochal accord with Czechoslovakia resolving 51-year-old American claims to certain Moravian pitchblende deposits. Failure to negotiate this agreement could have conceivably prompted a Czech invasion of West Germany and Austria, thus precipitating a devastating world war.

Indeed, our Administration has signed more agreements with more foreign countries than the last six Presidents combined. How have we achieved such an extraordinary record of success? A conceptually bold new U.S. "chain treaty," devised by a member of the First Family before her recent marriage, has been extremely helpful. The White House estimates that so far, some 700 world leaders and ministerial officials have been sent photocopies of the generic U.S. document, the text of which follows:

"Dear Foreign Leader:

Greetings, friend. You have been chosen to receive this peace treaty from the United States Government, just as many of your predecessors have. THIS IS NOT A JOKE. DO NOT DESTROY THIS TREATY! The last two recipients who did throw it away—the Shah of Iran and Yuri Andropov—died soon afterward. Maurice Bishop of Grenada thought the treaty he received last summer was a Jamaican prank. Earlier this year, Syrian President Hafez Assad scoffed at his treaty, then suffered a severe heart attack.

This treaty has been circulating among world leaders for almost two years, but its roots go back centuries, to James Monroe and

Not the war in Vietnam: Uninformed critics harp on the idea that helping embattled Central American democracies is a repeat of the mishandled involvement in Southeast Asia. The facts show otherwise. In Vietnam, troops were frequently transported in helicopters with two propellers, whereas in Central America the single-rotor models are preferred. Vietnam also had a lot of water buffaloes; you don't find any at all in El Salvador. And what's more, Vietnam was next to the South China Sea, and, in contrast, Central America's sandy beaches face the sunny Caribbean on one side and the mighty Pacific on the other.

After a fact-find-ing tour of their neighborhood by Secretary of State George Shultz, resi-dents of Dacca, Bangladesh, demon-strate their pro-Ameri-can spirit by launching a three-day search for the Secretary's left contact lens. The lens didn't turn up, but U.S. officials arranged for each searcher to receive two kilos of fresh rubbish and a book of matches embossed with the State Department seal.

the ancient Greeks. Do you sincerely want peace? This treaty has worked wonders for many countries—now yours could be one of them! But you must not tell a soul that you have received it. It is a *secret* treaty between your country and the United States.

Make four copies of the treaty. Sign one copy and mail it to Great Keeper of the Mis-sives, State Department, Washington, D.C. Then add your name to the list of world lead-ers below, and mail one copy to each of the world leaders listed. DO NOT SEND CASH OR STAMPS! This is a binding international treaty, not a moneymaking scheme of any kind.

Hesitate not! Mail treaties within 48 hours or Andropov's fate may await you.
Sincerely,
The Government of the United States of America.''

Peasantries

Gabon. Suriname. Pakistan. To most Americans, they are just queer names on some map. To us too. But the Administration of Ronald Reagan regards them as bona fide countries, actual nations with their own little Governments, brightly colored paper money, Army uniforms—and millions, maybe *bil-lions*, of poor people. And poor people in developing countries, unlike poor people in a certain developed country, cannot just waltz downtown and trade in their welfare checks for drugs and videocassette recorders. The poor in Gabon and Suriname and Pakistan must sit half-naked in hot, dusty camps while flies land on their faces.

We want to help the truly needy overseas, even though they are of no strategic value to the U.S. And we intend to provide aid with-out exporting the kind of welfare dependency

" *Disraeli once said that those who forget history are condemned to repeat it. Now, Disraeli was a great British statesman, the only Jewish Prime Minister I believe they've ever had over there, and he certainly knew something about history first-hand—he was right in the middle of it! But what he said is also true today, perhaps more so. Why, when Chairman Khrushchev was visiting from Russia some years ago, and he asked to go and visit Disneyland—of all the places he could go, he picked Disneyland—I remember my boss at General Electric at the time, Ed McKenna—Ed asked me if I'd go out to Anaheim as G.E.'s sort of 'foreign minister,' to be out there at the G.E. pavillion when Khrushchev came around. I said, 'Sure, Ed, but tell me one thing—if he tells me he's going to "bury me," do I have to hand him the shovel?'*

Well, that was just a joke, of course. But the principle of my remark to Ed McKenna remains valid to this very day, and it is what I use to guide my conduct of America's policy overseas. Some of our critics in Congress seem to want us to say to the Soviet Union, 'Do whatever mischief around the world that you like—just don't tell us about it!' That reminds me of some parents I remember who didn't care if their kids got in all kinds of trouble at school, or wherever, as long as they never heard about it. And there you have the kind of thinking that led one of England's Prime Ministers who maybe wasn't so great as Disraeli—Neville Chamberlain—that led Chamberlain to appease Adolf Hitler in Munich in 1938, and then the Nazis just kept going, through Poland and all, through Europe. The 1940s happened to be wonderful years for me personally, but it was a bum time for many people in the world—there again, they were condemned to forget their history. "

From Marxist Nicaragua, definitive evidence of Havana's deep involvement in the affairs of the country. This photograph, showing a Nicaraguan army platoon hunting down priests and advocates of democracy, was taken near the city of Matagalpa by an anti-Sandinista journalist who got his camera and film entirely on his own—not under CIA direction.

invented by Democratic Party theorists. Foreign aid does not have to be "thrown at the problem." Rather, it can be filtered very slowly to needy countries—and then, if we want, we can snap it back at the last second, just for laughs or to teach the ungrateful foreign leaders a lesson.

There is one innovative program that makes us proud above all the rest. Remember the old CARE package with seeds, trowels, blankets and the like? We think that kind of charity is just fine—for peasants who don't mind *staying* peasants. The Reagan Administration envisions instead a world in which a South Korean kale farmer can become a world-respected pantyhose manufacturer, in which a poor Chilean copper miner can start his own securities brokerage, in which an illiterate Nepalese widow will rent her 17 children to a carnival and get rich investing the profits in Arizona real estate.

If the world's poor are to step out of the shackles of poverty and into the exciting world of free enterprise, they're going to need some help. And that's precisely what our Business In A Box program aims to do. No saws and powdered milk wrapped in a brown paper package. Rather, Business In A Box recipients (23,701 men and women in 48 terrible little countries this fiscal year) find on the doorstep of their huts a handsome vinyl attaché case shipped direct from America—and that's enough to make most of them happy for the rest of their lives. Inside is practically everything anybody needs to start a business of his own: a calculator (which can be programmed to play several simple melodies), a dozen "I Like Ike" yellow legal pads, 100 fill-in-the-blank business cards, an official WPA mechanical pencil and a handy booklet explaining leveraged buyouts in English, Sudanese, Hindi and Spanish. In addition, along with every 10th kit we are shipping a top hat and Chamber of Commerce charter. According to field reports, one enthusiastic recipient in Senegal is planning to franchise his mud delivery business throughout sub-Sahara Africa, and a family of Brazilian Indians used its Business In A Box to start its own pulp boutique. It's free enterprise—and, courtesy of Ronald Reagan and America, it's truly free.

Good Conditions

Our Administration has generally opposed making foreign aid contingent on a Government's observing so-called human rights standards. Placing such conditions on aid *selectively*, we believe, is both counterproductive and patronizing. However, beginning January 1, the President has decreed the following *across-the-board* conditions for receiving U.S. grants and credits:

☐ At all official dinners, receptions and other functions attended by U.S. personnel in a foreign country, California white wines must be served at a temperature not less than 38°F and not more than 44°F, and no smelly foreign cheeses are to be made available.

☐ When referring to the U.S. in public, foreign officials of ministerial rank or higher must use the modifiers "wonderful" or "fabulous," e.g., "We are receiving only a little military assistance from the *fabulous* U.S. government."

☐ At least 3 percent of the country's total land area (no less than 1.2 million contiguous acres) are to be defoliated and turned into a lizard habitat called the Loyal Davis Memorial Fun Park.

WE, THE PEOPLE #4

We like the American country, the American government and the President and his magnificent spouse, Mrs. Nancy Reagan! My people should refer to me as "the President John F. Kennedy of the Philippines," because we are Catholic and, like President Kennedy, I was born in the year 1917 and have done many great things for my country—destroying Communism, for example! Still I am most in the debt of Ronald Reagan.

Here is my 19th year in which I am privileged to serve as head of state. I know President Reagan is the friend of the Philippines, because he has 1) given us many good millions of dollars for our defense against Communists, 2) had the American intelligence help to lose and find the man who says he is my daughter's husband, and 3) arranged that I would play golf in the 1983 Glenn Campbell Classic tournament in California! For those benefits I was very thankful. Therefore, when President Reagan decided not to visit my country in 1983, I understood it was because public relations were not auspicious at the time!

Soon I will begin the third decade of my office-holding as President Reagan will begin his second term of office-holding. Thus we are the same. We will be guiding the Philippines and America together down a friendly path, together devastating Communism and together advancing on a rainbow over the Pacific, even without the elections.

Defense
Pentagon: Now It's Back

By now you've read about some of the exciting goings on here at USCO. You have read about our fight to deregulate pollution, to extend the rights of the unborn to all mammals and to protect illegal aliens by allowing their sale to the rich. And as proud as we are of these achievements, as impressive as they sound, we know that deep down inside you couldn't care less. We know the real reason you put your trust in the present management. We know what you really want from us, what you've always wanted. Because we share your dream. It's an old dream, a dream that went so far out of fashion that in recent years you feared even to express it aloud lest you be ridiculed by the old crowd that used to run things and by their craven followers. They said it was impossible. They said it was too dangerous to ever try again. They said we had to have *parity*, and *coexistence*, and *détente*. But you always knew better, didn't you? That's why you chose us. Because you knew that we weren't too scared to make the dream come true.

We're going to *win*.

The proud and mighty battleship New Jersey continues her glorious tradition as the flagship of America's new fleet of space weapons. Placed into orbit along with an entire convoy of World War II vintage warships, the New Jersey is just one example of how the Administration is saving money by making the most out of our existing arsenal.

The Best Defense

Nothing in the business world is as exciting as seeing a sick concern fight its way back to tip-top health. That's why we at USCO are proud of what we call the Military Miracle.

Just a couple of years ago, Americans were wondering where our world-famous Pentagon had gone. It seemed that any pack of flea-bitten, mouth-frothing camel drivers could trample Old Glory in the dust and not even have to worry about getting napalmed. Well, those days are over! The defense rests no more. Not since we put the force back in Armed Forces.

Defense chief Cap Weinberger knows that you can't sit around waiting for peace—you have to go out and fight for it. So he and President Reagan have sent our men in uniform to wage peace all over the world. As the President recently told the Joint Chiefs, "Boys, defense is fine. But there's nothing offensive about offense, either."

Military Drills

The defense community began to buzz with excitement this year when we unveiled our fabulous spring collection of strategic arms. To the sound of wild applause from the critics and gnashing teeth in Moscow, one striking piece after another came dancing off the drawing boards and into deployment. Western creativity had triumphed again.

Of course the glamour item was the marvelously inventive Earthworm, the only missile that sits upside down in its silo. We've always been strong in the air, on land and at sea—now for the first time we're tough underground! That's because Earthworm, with its six-foot titanium-drill warhead, burrows straight through the earth, bypassing the enemy's radar and his air defenses. Then, about two weeks after all the other nukes have petered out and the enemy thinks things are quieting down—POW!—Earthworm comes

In a moving ceremony, the Commander-in-Chief awards a Purple Heart to Army Sgt. Frank Yuntz. The valiant hero neutralized an entire regiment of Mauritanian commandos—single-handedly.

through the basement and delivers a surprise kick in the butt.

Because Earthworm must drill through rock 20 times harder than the head of a certain well-known Congressional leader from the opposition party, the missiles cost $4.9 billion each. Hardly too much to pay, especially since the tunnels made by Earthworm make natural fallout shelters in the event of enemy retaliation. Not bad for the most "boring" missile ever devised!

But Earthworm wasn't our only spring sensation. Also winning plaudits was the stunning new Cockroach. A triumph of miniaturiza-

New U.S. intermediate-range nuclear weapons have been deployed in Western Europe with a maximum amount of discretion. Can you find the missiles in this picture? We sure can't.

A drill-tipped missile blasts through a rock formation in the Saudi Arabian desert 129 hours to the second after it was launched from a Nevada testing range.

Lovely U.S. Marine Jo Anne Quigley catches some rays on a sandy Canary Island beach. Disguised as an innocent California girl traveling the world in search of the "endless summer," Jo Anne was able to accurately call in artillery target coordinates to U.S. warships during the amphibious assault on that strategic land mass.

tion, this missile is only 16 inches long and carries a quark-bomb warhead that produces the cutest little nuclear blast you ever saw— its mushroom cloud rises only three feet!

If Cockroach is so tiny, where's its punch, you ask? Why, in its numbers. More than 350 million will be built and deployed, allowing us to launch the thrilling new concept called Total Guaranteed Individual Decommunization. First suggested to Nancy Reagan by singer Pat Boone at a White House gala, TGID ensures that in the event of major conflict, every single Soviet Communist will be eliminated. How? Simple. Detailed satellite photography has enabled us to identify all Russian citizens and to keep them under constant surveillance. Each and every Commie has been individually targeted with his or her

Defense? Sure, I'm all for it! I remember the story of one man who went into combat with his platoon, and before long he saw every last one of his buddies hit, even the guy he grew up with in the same town who played the harmonica. But you know, he was the last thing to stand between the enemy and the shores of America, in a sense. So he just stood up and fought, with no regard for his own life. And he won, and later was awarded a Congressional Medal of Honor.

That's why a strong defense is so important to this country, and why I've seen that movie at least a dozen times.

own Cockroach missile. So it doesn't matter where you run, Ivan—there's a Cockroach with your name on it.

Just as Cockroach heralds a new era of strategic conflict, it also provides a hands-on opportunity for the American worker. The missile's simple design means that anyone with a few tools and a workshop in his garage can become a home-grown defense contractor. Bidding on the $1.5 million contracts is open to anybody—and that especially includes minority businessmen.

Spatial Effects

When shrewd investors talk military biz these days, the hot action is in space. Everyone's heard about our highly publicized Star Wars Defense. Plans for it are forging ahead despite Congress's recent refusal to fund the program. But since the Star Wars Defense, with its Tom Cruise antisatellite missiles and its impenetrable Brooke Shields, won't be deployed until the spring of 2236, we've rushed some interim space weapons into action to beat the Russkies to the cosmic punch.

Nothing has captured the public's fancy as much as our recent dedication of Fort John Wayne, the first defense outpost on the moon. Muttering by leftish media grouches that there was no military threat to the moon quickly subsided when CIA satellites snapped photos of discarded vodka bottles in several strategic craters. Now with our astromarines defending the lunar landscape, Ivan will have to think twice. As comedian Bob Hope put it in his surprise visit to the desolate but gritty outpost last Christmas, "Don't worry—no Commie's going to moon us."

Deploy's the Thing

Bombs are a grand old American tradition. Why, even our national anthem proudly hails "the bombs bursting in air." So our R&D boys always try to come up with some provocative new bombs, and this year we produced two solid winners:

☐ The Quiet Bomb: The Q Bomb should come in very handy for all those covert wars the

CIA gets us into. The trouble is that they become uncovert all too quickly. Why? All that roaring noise from bombs, mines and missiles gives the game away—and is our face red! The "Q" packs all the power of conventional bombs but explodes without the telltale boom, just a wimpy "pfft" type of sound. Quiet Bombs blow up with utmost discretion. Enemy personnel will be totally stumped as they fly into the air without their legs.

□ The Neuter Bomb: A very subtle and interesting weapon, the Neuter Bomb does not damage property or cause conventional injury but will make target personnel sterile. Our defense planners aren't yet sure exactly how the Neuter Bomb will fit into our strategic picture, but they do contemplate large income from the sale of this bomb to India and China, whose Governments have expressed interest in using it on their own populations.

Marines à la Mode

One of the biggest security problems now facing the U.S., our allies, clients and subsidiaries is the growing popularity of terrorism.

Before he even knew what hit him, Muscovite Ilya Andbrezneko was blown apart by one of our devilish individually targeted nuclear projectiles. Each and every Soviet citizen has one of these babies with his name on it. Ilya got what was coming to him after he made an obscene gesture to one of our surveillance satellites.

But that's no reason to be terrified. We've found that even the nastiest terrorists can be knocked off-balance with a little creative thinking. That's why, for instance, we made the controversial but brilliant move of converting the U.S. Marines into a plainclothes service.

Remember when all those Marines were blown up by a truck bomb during the recent unpleasantness in Beirut? Well, the whole problem was that sitting there all bunched up in one building in their proud Marine uni-

WE, THE PEOPLE #5

I own a small hardware store just north of Fort Dix. It's just a small shop, nothin' fancy, and I've always made a good livin' from it.

The other day, I'm sweepin' the floor and this five-star general comes rushin' in here. "Gimme a screw," he barks, "and make it snappy." Well, I could tell this guy wasn't the type to take second-rate merchandise, so I give him the best we had—titanium alloy, laser-bore molding, the works. He takes it, hands me his card, says "Send the bill here."

Well, that's exactly what I did. Next month, I get a U.S. Government check for $187,000! I taped it to the front of the register for a few days, just for conversation, then decided I should send it back and straighten this whole mess out.

Ten days later, I get another check back—for $187,535! And there's a note saying that's the going rate for screws nowadays. Then a guy in a big tank pulls in for some pliers—this time they paid in cash, a stack of brand new hundreds straight from the mint! Damn if that don't beat all!

Well, like I said, this is a small operation, but I'm makin' a good livin' from it.

forms, our boys were sitting ducks. Next time they go into a Beirut-type occupation, the Marines will be dressed as tourists and carry their weapons in their luggage or hidden under their bathing suits. And rather than cluster up in one easily blasted building, they'll check into hotels and motels in small groups. The terrorists won't know who our Marines are till they come out shooting!

True, there have been complaints that dressing Marines in mufti violates a hallowed tradition. But we quickly solved that problem by commissioning world-famous designer and real manly kind of guy Ralph Lauren to work up some spiffy camouflage-pattern leisure suits, sport jackets and jeans for our fighting leathernecks.

As an added measure of protection, a scientific nutrition program has been designed to build up the immunity of our fighting forces to chemical weapons. The nation's largest fast-food chains are donating their fine food products, most of which contain large amounts of the same chemicals used in enemy weapons.

Death Is a Salesman

As we introduce new improved missiles like Earthworm and Cockroach, what becomes of our reliable Titans and Minutemen?

Why, we'll reap enormous profits selling them to impoverished nations at our Ordnance Resale Centers, which recently opened to booming business in 16 different locations around the globe. According to Pentagon marketing projections, we'll have no trouble selling out our entire inventory of outmoded strategic nuclear weapons. Revenues from our nuclear "fireball sale" will cover much of the estimated acquisition cost of an updated nuclear first-strike capability.

Not only Governments but also guys in dark glasses with briefcases full of greenbacks have been snapping up these still sturdy models which for so long stood guard over the Free World. Sure, they're a little rusty, and sometimes a launch button sticks or a silo cover jams, but for dollar-value our goodies are miles ahead of those big, expensive, sol-id-fuel-guzzling clunkers the Russians have been trying to unload as "the Cadillac of missiles." Plenty of eyebrows were raised in the Middle East last month when a Soviet SS-16 Shtarker missile sold to Iraq for use against the Iranians detonated on launch, totally annihilating the populace of Baghdad. "No more Red lemons for us," vowed Iraq's Chief of Staff. "From now on we shop at USCO."

Atom Antiques

We do have some nukes on hand that are too old to do the job—after all, we've been in the business longer than anyone else. But even our earliest models have profit potential —in fact, they've become collector's items. For instance, our original Hiroshima Hotfoot models circa 1945—only six are left—are now the Fabergé eggs of nuclear weapons. Our experts appraise them at $145 million each. These and other old-timers are on sale at our swank Boutique de Nuques in Paris, where they've caused a sensation among the chic international set.

There's more to the arms biz than nukes. We sell every kind of armament you can name, from hand grenades to submarines to economical Saturday night specials.

One of our most popular items is the new American Army Spoon, a pocket-sized wonder containing in one small tool every implement needed for modern-day survival. The folding spoon includes a cordless telephone, stereo headphones, a hot-wiring car-starter tool, a corkscrew, a condom and, of course, a heavy-duty coke spoon.

And don't forget our Computer Enemy Matching. This helpful service is for clients who buy our arms but can't seem to find an attractive foe to use them against. We provide the name of a country you can attack and defeat and thus train your forces and stir up a little patriotism among your citizens to boot. One satisfied customer, Margaret Thatcher of Great Britain, writes, "Without Computer Enemy Matching, we never would have thought of going against the Argentines. Fabulous!"

USCO: The Corporation
The Government of America is Business

Our vision for USCO is crystal clear: We seek to privatize the public sector, without publicizing or presenting in any embarrassing way our private sector. After all, we're the same people who took the Free out of Free Enterprise. Now we're taking the Government out of Big Government.

Following an exhaustive analysis of the assets of what used to be known as the United States Government, management quickly moved to restructure its operations to maximize the profit potential of each division. The result: a streamlined high-technology company specializing in security services. But we're also a diversified enterprise, with major holdings in consumer products, entertainment, leisure time and many of the other growth areas of the 1980s.

Your company is now poised to seize the enormous profit-making opportunities of the coming four years and beyond. The era of glad-handing, kowtowing, handshaking and baby kissing is behind us. Now we're going to show them that USCO *means* business.

USA
IN THE NEWS

We're the people
who put the *good* back in news.

Vanity Fair, September 1984

Everybody's talking about...Ronald Reagan

He's funny, he's cute, he rides horses, he's really cool and he's running for president again on the ticket with the elephants on it. With any luck, he'll make it to next year's swank Inaugural Ball (that's in January—the *coolest* month, you know). We love him, and we think his policies have pizazz.

JEWISH DAILY FORWARD   *May 1, 1984*   K7

"Why I Love Ronald Reagan"

by Isaac Bashevis Singer

It was many thousands of years ago, when I was a small boy growing up in a shtetl in Poland, that I first discovered the Republican Party. Then they were a tiny underground group composed mainly of radicals and building superintendents. Today, in New York where

I live, work and consume large quantities of kippered salmon, the Republicans are now a broad coalition, including Jewish people and the like. (Let me add here that Barbra Streisand is not a Republican.) For this and 42 other reasons, each equally valid, I am a Ronald Reagan supporter—as well as a Jew, of course!

Jewish Daily Forward, May 1, 1984

VARIETY
INTERNATIONAL
30

Jane Makes It Plain: Ron's Her Game

Wyman Nixes Fritz, Sez Jesse's Messy

Hollywood—"Falcon Crest" star Jane Wyman gives nod to boffo Prexy candidate Ron Reagan Sr. in video confab this ayem.

WWD
WOMEN'S WEAR DAILY
MONDAY, APRIL 30, 1984
VOL. 147 NO. 84
50 Cents

WINNING FALL LINE

Wearing a grey pin-stripe jacket and an oh-so-white shirt and red tie with blue dots, President Ronald Reagan took his first steps down the Republican plank last night as part of the Reagan fall campaign. Close behind him was the slightly more dashing sidekick, George Bush, dressed in a natty blue suit and a surprisingly witty bow tie. The fact that he was wearing a short-sleeved shirt didn't seem to faze the potential buyers, who scurried backstage afterward for a peek at the Reagan undergarments.

Variety, July 8, 1984

Women's Wear Daily, April 30, 1984

TOWN & FOREIGN COUNTRY

THE MAGAZINE OF THE U.S. DIPLOMATIC CORPS

Vol. 1 No. 1/AUGUST 1983

ESTABLISHED 1983

On our cover: Contemporary beauty and Administration wife of the month Barbara Bush.

Top Secrets

BY SELWA ROOSEVELT

Dear D.C.: Ciao again from funny old Foggy Bottom, American ladies and gentleman…Heard a marvelous one last evening at that sweet Swede Willy Wachtmeister's embassy affaire: What do Undersecretaries for Political Affairs eat for lunch? A big fat Eagleburger—but hold the Russian! (I nearly died I kled so hard)…What wrinkly delegate to the United Nations so many Scotch-and-sodas the ight at Bill and Pat Buckley's he practically begged a certain ary of Defense up to her Waldorf for some frank and fruitful nge? (I'm not telling)…Fun It seems our new, nicer depart-ment will spend more this fiscal year on butter knives than on all non-military aid to Bangladesh and Pakistan combined! (Maybe next year India could grow some of its own wheat so we could finally buy some decent crystal for the embassy residences…)

In Continent: One doesn't want to say Obie Shultz dresses badly, but I could have **sworn I** saw the Secretary waltzing with a big old bag of dog food at the International Atomic Energy Agency Ball in Vienna a fortnight ago …Seems we may not pull out of that anti-American UNESCO after all—no point in leaving **Paris** because of some snit over censorship…When In Rome Department: Ambassador Max Rabb may not take communion, but he was **Mister Vino** recently. His party for 30 Roman couples (and a few cardinals) went through eight cases of Lafite-Rothschild '61—the lot of it drunk straight from the bottles with straws. I mean, **marvelous!**

Quotation of the Day

"Yes." President Reagan, in response to a question at yesterday's news conference.
August 5, 1984

Minutiae

flea outbreak threa'
ndi's pig farme'

INTERVIEW WITH THE PRESIDENT

With guest journalists Roger Mudd, NBC News; Seymour Hersh, freelance writer; Ted Koppel, ABC News; Joan Lunden, "Good Morning, America"; and Walter Cronkite.

MUDD: Welcome, Mr. President. Would you mind doing your Teddy Kennedy imitation for us?

REAGAN: Not at all, Roger. (pause) "Mary Jo, I can't see where I'm going. Is that a parking space? WHOAAA!!! HELP!"

LUNDEN: Yes sir, thank you. Where did you get those alligator cowboy boots?

REAGAN: Joan, I thought you were all warned about asking those kind of questions--I can't answer that!

MUDD: Mr. President, can you tell the difference between mauve and fuchsia?

REAGAN: Fourteen.

MUDD: I see.

KOPPEL: Mr. President, why haven't you withdrawn American support for the rebels in Nicaragua?

REAGAN: Ted, I'm pleased you're giving me the chance to respond to that. (pause) Joan?

HERSH: Mr. President, are you deaf?

REAGAN: What?

MUDD: Thank you, Ron.

REAGAN: Yes.

KOPPEL: A follow-up question. Where do you get your cowboy boots?

REAGAN: Yes.

HERSH: Mr. Reagan, do you plan to keep George Bush as your running mate this year?

REAGAN: Do you mean George Bush the vice president?

HERSH: Yes I do.

REAGAN: Thank you. Usually no one notices.

KOPPEL: Sir, has anyone ever told you that you look like Jack Lord?

REAGAN: Yes, Nixon said that to me. He advised me to run for Governor of Hawaii.

CRONKITE: Yes, Mr. President. May I ask you a question?

REAGAN: Yes, fire away.

CRONKITE: Do you feel, as I do, that the quality of television news has dropped dramatically in recent years; to the point where Americans can get less information from the network news shows than from the front page of their daily newspaper, a result of an emphasis on anchormen instead of news coverage?

REAGAN: Well, Ted--I mean, Rog--I mean, Sy--excuse me, uh, David....

Presidential news conference, December 19, 1983

President Reagan, in a Dramatic Move, Said to Change Hair Color, Bicep Size; Aides Celebrate Surprise Policy Coup

By BRUCE
Special to The New York Times

This morning, the White House [...] a form[...] [...]nt of regret

The New York Times, March 4, 1982

Byte, June 1981

OVERBYTES

Rewritten press releases of the microcomputer industry

REAGAN SOLVES NICARAGUAN CRISIS WITH PCjr!

Thanks to his OBM QC7 program and a compu-compatible machine with semi-digital conductors, Ronald Reagan was able to successfully negotiate a settlement with Nicaraguan rebels and squeeze in a game of "Space Invaders" before going to bed one night last week. Naturally, the President had made certain that his computer equipment was compatible with those owned by other world leaders, and his close advisers recommended the PCjr over any other machine. "You can solve most world problems on this console in less than three minutes," Constantin Chernenko, the Premier of the Soviet Union, recently told the Politburo," and plus you can get one for 3000 rubles and change."

The Washington Post, August 9, 1984

Mondale Endorses Reagan

By Martin Scram

Baltimore, Md.—Emmanuel Mondale, a state assemblyman from the Southwest Side, yesterday endorsed Ronald Reagan's election campaign. Mr. Mondale offered this reason for the endorsement: "He paid me."

Tuesday, May 1, 1984

Farrakhan Calls Reagan "Best World Leader Since Hitler"

Muhammad Ali Farrakhan, our spiritual leader and hired gun, has told his followers they should vote for Ronald Reagan in the 1984 campaign. "Mr. Reagan has assured me that he is a racist," Farrakhan told reporters as he left a White House meeting yesterday, "and I believe him." Mr. Farrakhan explained that the best way for black people to achieve power in this country is to have all but he and Jess Jackson killed. Then, he said, "they'll have to give us good jobs, out of guilt."

Muslim Digest, May 1, 1984

Crossword Television
6B 5D

USA PAPSHOTS

Yet another batch of dumb statistics

We're better off!

Average number of Americans better off today than they were four years ago.

- Women named Sidney 57%
- White 78%
- Polish 67%
- Polynesian 83%

Source: *Better Homes & Gardens*

USA Today, January 15, 1983

Why I Believe in the Environment

By Sandy Duncan

As we were going to press, Sandy Duncan's short but extremely crunchy and slightly salty life came to a tragic end. Other celebrities have drowned. Some others have fallen down and hit their heads. Sandy was found at the bottom of Topanga Canyon, completely and totally plucked.

It's only natural that I was picked to be in that Wheat Thins commercial—the one where I was walking kind of pensively through a big field of wheat, holding a box of Wheat Thins. You see, I love all things in nature, not just wheat. I truly think I would have been just as happy doing a commercial for Rice Chex and wading through a rice paddy, except that I might have gotten my legs wet. Besides, you don't eat Rice Chex "one after the other," the way you do Wheat Thins. But my point is that I love fields. I'm not limited to one grain over another.

When I look back on it, it sometimes seems to me that my whole professional experience has been linked to the environment. Doing "Peter Pan" on Broadway, for instance. I think one of the reasons it was such a success—besides the fact that we all just had such a good *time* doing it—was that the flying scenes were so believable. We're all children inside, and I think we never lose that sense of wonder about flight. It represents that magical experience we'll never be able to have except in dreams. Even with all the guidewires, I really believed I was flying, and my joy was able to transmit itself to the audience.

That's why we must protect birds. We must never allow ourselves to live in a world where no one can fly, because then our dreams will die. Of course there would still be bats, and flying fish, but somehow they're not as inspiring. Birds are the ones who can really teach us lessons about themselves.

"Peter Pan" taught me other things about the environment, too. The character Peter is so natural. He doesn't want a job; he doesn't want to grow up; he doesn't even want to marry Wendy (which was just as well for me—I didn't have to do any kissing scenes!). All he really wants is just to stay a boy in Never-Never Land, 'cause growing up means it would be beneath his dignity to climb a tree. What he's saying is, "I don't want any part of your filthy cities and your polluting cars and your seal killings! I just want the freedom to be myself!" If we could all just stop and listen to our inner voices, I think we'd find that we were all saying the same thing.

I was so grateful when President Reagan appointed me to be Special Entertainment Chairman for the Department of Interior. And not only because I haven't worked in awhile. No, it was more because it gives me a chance to try and reach other people with my views about the environment, through performances of "Peter Pan" and maybe a lecture tour about the Wheat Thins commercial and what it means. I only hope I prove worthy of the President's trust in me.

In the Realm of the Census

By Malcolm Baldridge

Malcolm Baldridge heads one of the Government's key departments, the Department of Commerce. He makes many speeches and has even attended a Cabinet meeting! It's also kind of amusing that his last name, which includes the word "bald" and the word "ridge," is an ironic comment on his hairstyle.

The Bureau of the Census has been counting Americans for longer than anyone cares to remember. The work is extremely demanding for the thousands of census enumerators, tabulators and statisticians who must collect and organize billions of data every 10 years.

And we take our work seriously. Yet as required by the Department of Commerce Regulatory Revision 82-56, we also approach the Census task with a sense of adventure and good humor. Indeed, the logistics of our enterprise are so darn complicated that some small miscalculations are bound to creep in. That's why I thought it might be fun to share some "bloopers, boners and foulups" with you, the American people.

☐ Census Blooper #2486GR: Three years ago, a Census Bureau enumerator operating in district 16 of the Fayetteville-Springdale, Ark., Standard Metropolitan Statistical Area asked a respondent, "How many out-of-state trips, other than those for business, does the head of household take *anally*?" The enumerator, of course, had misspoken the word "annually." After everyone down at the local Bureau office had a good laugh over that one, the enumerator was suspended without pay and, following normal termination procedures, dismissed.

☐ Census Blooper #2431LW: The 1981-82 edition of *Statistical Abstract of the United States* incorrectly reported that there were only 4,300 infant deaths during 1981! The true number, of course, was 43,000. Although not a humorous error to most laypeople, that goof-up livened up the experts in the Bureau's Mortality Section for weeks.

☐ Census Blooper #2592PY: During 1981, one respondent in the Visalia-Tulare-Porterville, Cal., SMSA, misunderstood the enumerator's question regarding the household's number of flush toilets. Instead of answering, the respondent simply nodded and ran upstairs where he disconnected and destroyed his two toilets.

☐ Census Blooper #2633MH: This was one of the bureau's rare "double boners." In 1982 at a residence in the Lorain-Elyria, Ohio, SMSA, only one juvenile, age seven, was at home. When asked how many unrelated persons resided at least eight months per year in the household, the juvenile answered, "about a million." As a result, the Lorain-Elyria SMSA was thought to have experienced a 486 percent population increase in two years. (Our amusement turned to chagrin, however, when Lorain County was consequently awarded $1.2 billion in extra Federal revenue-sharing funds.)

Management's Review of Operations

Consumer Products Group

In the first fiscal term, the Group entered into a series of licensing agreements with manufacturers of evening gowns, teacups, riding crops, support hose, prosthetic devices, ground-to-air heat-seeking missiles, feminine hygiene products and other consumer items for the use of the Nancy Reagan designer label. We project $1.2 billion in revenue from this source in the first year of Fiscal Term II. The Consumer Products Group has also started to use one of USCO's most underutilized assets—Federal employees. This skillful but shifty and indolent pool of unwilling labor has been redeployed to the plastic toy and novelty subsidiary of the Consumer Products Group, known for its fish-shaped thermometers, frisbees, hula hoops and digital toenail clippers. An estimated 75,000 Federal employees—most formerly with the now-dismantled bureaucracies of health, energy, education and welfare—work in our efficiently managed production facilities housed in converted Federal office buildings. We don't expect to make too much money off of these widgets—but 15,000 Federal workers have already quit or committed suicide, saving USCO millions by reducing pension obligations.

Entertainment Group

In a landmark agreement, USCO has acquired a controlling equity interest in each of the three major television networks. It's well known that the networks reap huge profits from their news programming, and USCO should share in those profits—for without us, there would be no news. At the same time, the Group has canceled its plans to hold marathon Presidential press conferences during the networks' critical ratings "sweep weeks." President and CEO Reagan will continue to be telegenic, affable, spontaneous, down-home, boyish and just like your grandpa before he was "put away." We have also entered into a deal with the American Broadcasting Company to create a television series entitled *Capitol Hill Street Blues,* the first "deficituation comedy."

High Society Group

The trend is clear. Over the past four years, advertisements in magazines, on billboards and on television have put it succinctly: It's okay, again, to be ambitious. It's okay, again, to want wealth. It's okay, again, to improve the quality of one's own life, so long as one is prepared to sacrifice the quality of someone else's. Because nothing worthwhile comes without sacrifice.

Not everyone will attain this newly legitimized success. In fact, no one will. But we believe that the struggle is as important as the fruits of victory—particularly when there is no victory, and there are no fruits. For then, indeed, the struggle is all. This is what is meant by the American Dream. But before there can be any dream-

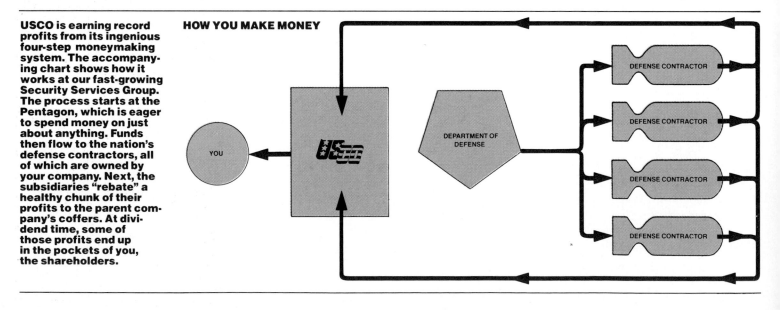

USCO is earning record profits from its ingenious four-step moneymaking system. The accompanying chart shows how it works at our fast-growing Security Services Group. The process starts at the Pentagon, which is eager to spend money on just about anything. Funds then flow to the nation's defense contractors, all of which are owned by your company. Next, the subsidiaries "rebate" a healthy chunk of their profits to the parent company's coffers. At dividend time, some of those profits end up in the pockets of you, the shareholders.

HOW YOU MAKE MONEY

YOU

DEPARTMENT OF DEFENSE

DEFENSE CONTRACTOR

DEFENSE CONTRACTOR

DEFENSE CONTRACTOR

DEFENSE CONTRACTOR

ing, there first must be falling asleep—and sleep, as scientists know, is self-hypnosis. Before there can be the Dream, there must be the Fantasy.

USCO was built on such a philosophy, and looks with zest to a future in which the very wealthy, the indubitably secure, and the really, really powerful resume their traditional role in American life as idols, as heroes, as demigods. The truly amazingly, stupendously rich must no longer be consigned to the hidden mansions of Newport and the ill-lit back streets of Beverly Hills. They must come "out of the walk-in closet" and resume their rightful place in society—not just "high society," but regular, everyday "low society." Some human beings are indeed capable of purchasing a Piaget wristwatch for $20,000 without guilt. It is time for those people to show the rest of America how.

But that is only the beginning. We plan to make use of this special portion of society by trumpeting, in all major media, their achievements, their homes, their interior decorations, their clothing, their salaries, their dinner, their shoes, their vacations and their wives. Nor will we stop there. We propose to convene, each month, at our expense, a gathering of the elite from the wealthiest sectors of society. These exemplars of success will commit their time and energies to a series of two-week symposia, aboard the world-famous Queen Elizabeth II, in an effort to address the question, "Why is money so great?" The results of these conferences will be published by the USCO Publishing Division and made available to schools, church groups and individuals for a nominal fee.

Financial Services Group

The highly profitable Federal Reserve Bank Division will continue to be highly profitable. At USCO, not only do we make money, but we *make* money. Management also expects to put the money-losing Social Security Insurance Division on a profitable footing. We've added flight insurance policies for air travelers to our array of policy offerings. Next, we plan to expand into the international insurance market with coverage protecting client nations against military coups, droughts and falling space debris.

Leisure Time Group

In partnership with the nation's leading natural resources companies, the Leisure Time Group plans to open hundreds of industrial theme parks throughout the country. Tourists will flock to these fun centers—located in what used to be unproductive national parks. Families can experience the hands-on thrill of being a "roughneck" drilling for oil, a miner tunneling deep below the earth for valuable minerals or a bulldozer operator at a strip mine.

The Leisure Time Group has also moved into the lucrative vacation time-sharing business. An offering of weekly vacation blocks in the glamorous Camp David Executive Retreat was sold out in a matter of hours. It was followed by an even more successful offering of time shares in the White House, which would have been totally unoccupied for more than 90 percent of Fiscal Term II. And the Group plans several new tourism promotion campaigns, following up on the success of its joint venture with Grenada's Tourist Bureau.

Democratic Party Group

Management sees little future potential in this troubled wholly owned subsidiary.

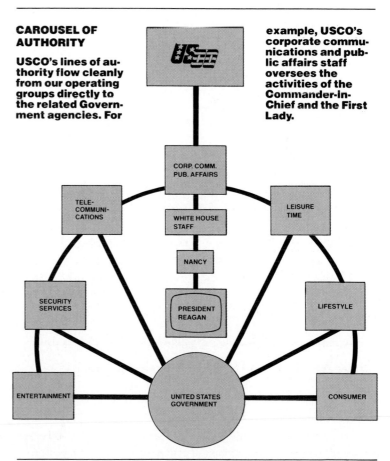

CAROUSEL OF AUTHORITY

USCO's lines of authority flow cleanly from our operating groups directly to the related Government agencies. For example, USCO's corporate communications and public affairs staff oversees the activities of the Commander-in-Chief and the First Lady.

Telecommunications Group

The Telecommunications Group has enjoyed considerable success with its new low-cost long distance communications link, particularly in the overseas phone call market. The new service—known as HOT-LINE—has put a red phone on the desks of some of America's most successful executives.

Security Services Group

In Fiscal Term I, management commenced the most massive capital investment program in the history of civilization, committing well over $1 trillion to a full range of state-of-the-art nuclear and conventional weapons. Naturally we have no plans whatsoever to actually use these awesomely beautiful creations. Instead, USCO's strategy for Fiscal Term II is designed so that we will receive a generous return on our massive investment, turning our Defense Division into a high-yield asset—not only in terms of sheer megatonage, but also in terms of yields that are bound to earn the respect and admiration of investors on every stock exchange and bourse in the entire world. Our theory is simple. We're going to start charging for a service we've been giving away for free for more than a quarter of a century. Not only have we been giving it away, but all we've gotten back in return is *grief*. For every $45 million tank we deploy in Western Europe, we get back an unfairly priced imported sports car. For every $450 million destroyer cruising in the Pacific, we get back 23,000 cheap digital watches made by a bunch of robots who get their kicks out of playing volleyball at 5 a.m. We're tired of making the world secure for the so-called friends who took all our free handouts and then turned right around to devote their lives to making us feel *insecure*. Starting on January 22, 1985, at exactly 12:01 a.m., we're gonna snap back that good old American strategic nuclear umbrella. Some of our allies may not care about getting wet, but maybe they don't know what it's like to get caught in a heavy downpour. Those who want to stay dry are going to pay for the pleasure. And we're gonna get back all our gold.

Note A—Acquisition of Businesses

In Fiscal Term I, USCO has moved aggressively to expand its worldwide market share. In the promising Central American market, both Honduras and El Salvador were brought into the USCO International Division through mergers involving an exchange of cash, stock, helicopters, condominium units and bananas. At the same time, we have continued to pursue our proxy fight with the entrenched management of Nicaragua. It has been a cardinal point at USCO since its inception that other companies must be free—free to produce in their own way, free to find their place in the community of trade and, most of all, free to become a wholly owned subsidiary of USCO. We are proud to reaffirm that view, and to back it with money, men and machine guns if necessary. Our longstanding joint-venture agreements with the management teams in place in the United Kingdom and Israel continue to generate substantial profits.

Note B—Competition

USCO's principal competitor in the world marketplace, MOSCO, has not wavered in its determination to force USCO out of business and dominate the world. That is why we have introduced a number of measures designed to respond in kind to the MOSCO threat. Not only have advances in weaponry enhanced our position on the retail level, but an all-out public relations campaign has been planned using major media to denounce, degrade and insult MOSCO as proof of our competitive zeal. In other competitive markets—namely the rest of the world—the THEMCO cartel continues to suffer from severe debt-related financial problems. Management is now considering a one-time leveraged buyout offer for THEMCO, which controls a small portion of the globe's productive assets, but well in excess of 84 percent of the world's arable land mass.

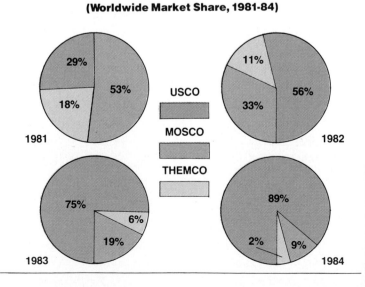

USCO vs. THEMCO & MOSCO
(Worldwide Market Share, 1981-84)

CONSOLIDATED STATEMENT OF INCOME

FISCAL TERM ENDED

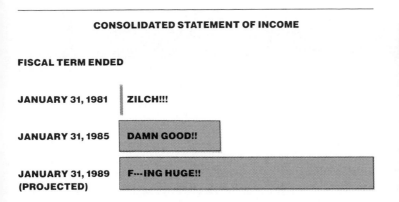

JANUARY 31, 1981	ZILCH!!!
JANUARY 31, 1985	DAMN GOOD!!
JANUARY 31, 1989 (PROJECTED)	F---ING HUGE!!

Note C—Investment in Affiliated Companies

USCO's Venture Capital Division has invested over $12 billion in a wide range of emerging growth companies. And in a series of fortuitous coincidences, it just so happens that all of these new concerns are operated by executives who were formerly at USCO!

Access Inc. Media organizations are always on the lookout for interviews with colorful Administration personalities. Access has become *the* hot Washington talent agency, putting together D.C. stars with reporters hungry for news. Former National Security Director Richard Allen is the superagent behind this venture.

Market Pulse Investment. In today's fast-paced investment climate, investors can ill afford to be the last to know about developments in the corporate world. Market Pulse guarantees that its clients will be the first to know what's happening, specializing in advance, exclusive information on corporate takeover bids. Investment pros Paul Thayer, formerly of the Department of Defense, and Max Hugel, who served briefly at CIA, head MPI's team of professionals.

Lab Animal Supply Corp. Medical research has a virtually insatiable appetite for animals to be used in the search for the cure of deadly diseases. Specializing in animals that most people would consider household pets, LAS is known for providing subjects with an unusually high threshold of pain, with vocal chords removed prior to shipping to prevent purring, barking and other cute noises. Former Secretary of the Interior James Watt is chairman and chief executive officer.

Toxiderm Inc. An acne medication containing chemicals that are too effective to throw out! The ultimate face saver, brought to the teenagers of America by Rita Lavelle, who once made headlines at EPA.

Report of Independent Accountants

To the Stockholders and Directors of USCO, Inc.

In our opinion, the accompanying financial report and statements represent an apparently and convincingly positive assessment of the financial position of USCO, Inc., and its subsidiaries, with regard to the fiscal term 1980–84, as ascertained by us using normal and acceptable auditing, concealment, and obfuscatory procedures as deemed necessary by us, the directorship of USCO, and everyone's attorneys.

USCO (formerly "The Government of the United States of America") is a corporation producing legislation, tax breaks, weapons, "favors," advanced technology, surplus cheese, pamphlets on how to build a soap-box racer, ungrown agricultural products, research into the wartime utility of psychic frogs, public denials, marching bands, nerve gas, covert intervention services, "Cold War" rhetoric, money, minor scandals, entitlements payments, and other goods and services.

Our findings confirm, or at least give every appearance of confirming, that, during Fiscal Term I, USCO earned substantial profits in both domestic and overseas markets, both as a broker acting as intermediary for the sale of weapons, durables, high-technology items, and baby formula, and as a direct provider of military goods and services (troops, "advisers," weaponry, ordnance, propaganda, materiel, public condemnation of right-wing terror, private tolerance of right-wing terror, etc.).

All such profits, advances, and positive developments are faithfully recorded and verified herein. Any losses, retreats, mistakes, errors, fumbles, miscues, or acts destined to assure future catastrophe may be examined in Special Section G of this report, not included herein and, in fact, nonexistent.

Coward, Craven and Trembling

Coward, Craven and Trembling
Certified Public Accountants

The Best Future Ever!

Well, four more years. What are we going to do with them? America will keep on getting greater and greater like it used to be, only more convenient. But what else can we look forward to?

I'm planning for some R and R. I've earned a little rest. It's hard work running a whole country. There are more than a million of you out there, and just one of me! And now that I've gotten everything under control, it's time to just settle back and enjoy the view.

After all, I've done everything I set out to do. The country's sure back on course again, and we're not bowing down to a Communist God the way we used to. I understand, from what they tell me, that "God" and "phooey" are the same word in Russian, and that Russian leaders tell their people that God is a big purple man with 50 fingers. So there's no doubt we're in better, safer hands now.

But it's been tough—my brain's had to work overtime. And Nancy's always telling me that the best leader is one who knows how to let the young go-getters do the work for him. The nation is a business now, as people keep explaining to me, and I'm leaving it in good hands. I've approved the appointment of 150 vice presidents—three for each state—to serve you better. They're all top men, I hear. They'll report to the Senior Vice President of Communications, who in turn reports to the Executive Vice President of Marketing and Military Affairs. And those are the fellows who will report to me if there's something they feel I should know about. Why, they're even authorized to knock when Nancy has flicked on the flashing amber light over the bedroom door!

I'll continue to oversee a few of the nation's most vital projects, the ones that are so important that only a Commander-in-Chief could handle them. Take the Presidential Time Capsule, for instance. This was my own idea, and I must confess I'm proud of it. What we're doing is building a steel safe under the Washington Monument. Then, inside,

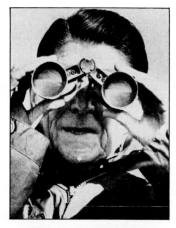

A new observation deck on the White House roof and a pair of special high- resolution binoculars will help the President keep an eye on things.

"Come any closer and I'll saw your arms off!" the President will playfully say to pushy aids who try to ruin his vacations at the Rancho Del Cielo.

At an upcoming disarmament conference, the President expects to surprise the delegates by having hundreds of bushes planted in the center of the conference table. A secret button activated by the President will ignite the small trees, demonstrating the Biblical story of the burning bush. Note also that the President plans to look even more intelligent—and sort of Chinese—than he does now.

we'll place some items that would be especially important to me in the future. Like a flashlight if the electricity were to go out and an assortment of foreign candies for meeting with kings and other world leaders. When we open this capsule a year from now, it will tell historians an awful lot about what the Reagan Presidency stands for.

These are some of the highlights of your Government's future. What about mine personally? Well, I've got a lot of ideas simmering on the back burner. This is one old gray mare who's not just trotting off to the glue factory! And neither is Nancy. We'll still be around and still be on TV a lot—we'll just be doing different types of appearances from now on.

For instance, I very much wanted to go to England's magnificent Royal Wedding, you know, but Ed Meese said it would look too—well,"faggoty" was the word Ed used, actually. So old Ron stayed home, going to lots of meetings in the middle of the hot Washington summer, and Nancy rides like Cleopatra in a horse-drawn motorcade, and attends the wedding of the century by herself. If I had gone they wouldn't have seated her way in the back next to a bunch of Icelanders. I guarantee

you, we would have been in the front row, me with the King and Nancy with the Queen. I keep worrying that the real reason neither of the other princes wanted to marry Patty is that Queen Elizabeth is still ticked off at me for not going. I'd probably have a daughter in Buckingham Palace now if I had stuck to my principles and gone. From now on, I can.

So there'll be a lot more of that. More state funerals, too, so I can wear my tuxedos. And a lot less of having to answer reporters' questions about why is Congress doing such and such or why some hoboes are starving to death in Chicago when anybody can see how much happier people are now. When they ask me that kind of attacking question from now on, I'll just put up my hands and say: "Easy, boys. You've only got to put up with it for four more years!" Then I'll wave and get into the helicopter.

I'd like to spend more time with my family, too. Gosh, I'll bet I haven't set eyes on Michael in 15 years! I see Maureen's picture in the papers sometimes, though, and she looks as though she's doing fine. Ron and Gloria—well, I don't need Mike Deaver to tell me they're probably better left alone. And Patty knows that if she changes her mind

Popular foreign leaders, top entertainers and even former Commanders-in-Chief will be invited to the White House to fill in as "Guest President of the Week." At an annual gala, President Reagan will present awards in many different categories of Presidential achievement.

President Reagan plans to keep a low profile, especially when nosy reporters ask trick questions that don't serve any useful purpose at all.

The President has agreed to appear as special guest star on some of America's favorite shows. That's going to require a lot of preparation, and the President plans to dine on frozen TV dinners so he can watch important programs while he eats with Nancy in the family quarters.

about the kind of fellow she thinks she wants, well, she's always welcome to visit us when we're alone at the ranch.

I also plan to concentrate a little bit on making a few more guest appearances on TV shows. Nancy's been representing the family in that area so far, but with my background, I'm sure I'll manage to keep from embarrassing my fellow Republicans! For instance, if we do go ahead and make the arrangements with *Love Boat*, the idea of the show could be that the President is taking a vacation cruise. They tell me I'd play the President. There could be jokes about national security matters, and girls in little bikini bathing suits would ask for my autograph. Then there will be one scene where I'm walking by the pool and a little boy splashes me by mistake. That little dickens is sure embarrassed. But I just chuckle and muss his hair, and everyone's relieved that I didn't make a big stink about it. It shows how human I am.

Most important to me, though, is a big decision I've made about my life. No matter how old you get, I think it's important not to just turn into a stump or something. We all keep changing; why, what if I'd decided just to stay a student at Eureka College. No, I can tell when I've reached a turning point. A time to make changes. And that's why I'm working on a different, better signature. When I sign things from now on, I want my handwriting to reflect the new me, the President. I haven't settled on just how it will be yet. But you may rest assured that my new John Hancock is a top priority for everyone in Government.

I'm styling my hair differently from now on, too. It was getting a little too tall.

So that's the future of America. Actually, it's kind of hard to believe that here I am writing this *now,* but you'll see it in the *future.* I don't quite understand the technicalities, but then that's not my job.

Have a wonderful future, and wish us a great time.

Ronald Ron Reagan

CREDITS

An USCO Parody, Inc., publication
**Produced by Bob Adelman, Peter Cohn
and David Kaestle.**

Editor: **Peter Cohn**

Contributing Editors: **Kurt Andersen, Fred Graver, Lewis Grossberger, Ann Hodgman, Ellis Wiener**
Associate Editor: **David Doty**
Assistant Editors: **David Blum, Prakash Mishra**
Copy Editors: **Tom Brown, Jessie Prichard Hunter**
Expatriate Editor: **Tony Hendra**

Art Director: **David Kaestle**

Original Photography: **Bob Adelman**
Production Supervisor: **Maggie Saliske**
Photographic Retouching: **Robert Rakita**
Illustration: **James Sherman**
Design Assistant: **Heather Gilchrist**
Prop Fabrication: **Chris Bobin, Lyndon Mosse, Maggie Saliske**
Photo Research: **Caroline Sheen**
Stock Photography Provided By: **FPG, Globe, Sygma, U.S. Government, UPI/Bettman Archive, Wide World Photos**